JOHN KILLEN was born in Belfast and was educated ~~at~~
Since 1977 he has been a librarian at the Linen Hall Li~~brary~~
exhibitions on a wide variety of themes, some of which ~~have~~ also been displayed in
the National Library of Ireland. He has lectured on library and historical subjects in
the USA and is a regular contributor to the *Linen Hall Review* and *Irish Booklore*. His
publications include *John Bull's Famous Circus, The Irish Christmas Book, The Pure
Drop: A Book of Irish Drinking, A History of the Linen Hall Library, The Famine Decade:
Contemporary Accounts, 1841–1851* and *The Decade of the United Irishmen:
Contemporary Accounts, 1791–1801*.

THE UNKINDEST CUT

A Cartoon History of Ulster
1900–2000

JOHN KILLEN

John Killen

THE
BLACKSTAFF
PRESS
BELFAST

First published in 2000 by
The Blackstaff Press Limited
Wildflower Way, Apollo Road
Belfast BT12 6TA, Northern Ireland

The acknowledgements on page ix constitute an extension of this copyright page

John Killen has asserted his right under the
Copyright, Designs and Patents Act 1988 to be identified
as author of this work

Printed in Ireland by ColourBooks

A CIP catalogue record of this book
is available from the British Library

ISBN 0-85640-682-1

to the memory of my mother
Bridie Killen, née Higgins
1923–2000

CONTENTS

ACKNOWLEDGEMENTS   IX

Overview   1

The Foundation of the State   7

A Protestant State for a Protestant People   32

Ulster at War   54

The Postwar Years   76

The Troubles 1969–2000   102

ACKNOWLEDGEMENTS

The author wishes to make grateful acknowledgment to the following individuals, newspapers and institutions whose help and co-operation have made this book possible:

The staff of the following libraries: the Linen Hall Library, Belfast; the National Library of Ireland; the Central Library, Belfast and the libraries of the South Eastern Education and Library Board.

News International Syndication for permission to reproduce cartoons by Gerald Scarfe from the *Sunday Times*, © Gerald Scarfe/Times Newspapers Limited, 2000; Express Newspapers for permission to reproduce cartoons by Giles from the *Sunday Express*; *Punch* for permission to reproduce cartoons by A.W. Lloyd, Bernard Partridge, Leonard Raven-Hill and the cartoons on pages 36 and 40; Yvonne Friers for permission to reproduce cartoons by Rowel Friers; the *Andersonstown News* for permission to reproduce cartoons by Oisín; the *Evening Standard* for permission to reproduce cartoons by JAK; the Students' Union, Queen's University Belfast, for permission to reproduce cartoons by Achie, D. Bell, J.T. Blair, Colm, Gianni, S. King, D. McG, MacNeil, Robert J. Marshall, Charles Nisbet, Jo Stewart and the cartoons on pages 42, 44, 49, 51, 52, 71 and 77, all from *PTQ*; the *Irish Independent* for the cartoon on page 14; *Constabulary Gazette* for permission to reproduce cartoons by R.J. McCullagh from *Guns in Ulster*, the Linen Hall Library for permission to reproduce the cartoons on pages 4, 23, 24, 26, 27 and 58; *An Phoblacht/Republican News* for permission to reproduce cartoons by Bob and Cormac; *Magill* for permission to reproduce the cartoon by Littleman; *Fortnight* for permission to reproduce the cartoon by Mark Hamilton; the *Spectator* for permission to reproduce cartoons by Michael Heath, Adam Singleton, Geoff Thompson and Richard Willson; Frank Kelly for permission to use the cartoons of Charles E. Kelly of *Dublin Opinion*; Mrs M. Campbell for permission to use the cartoons by George Campbell from *Ulster in Black and White*.

The author also wishes to express particular thanks to the following cartoonists for generously allowing their work to be reproduced: Steve Bell, Bob, Bernard Cookson, Cormac, Mark Hamilton, Michael Heath, Ian Knox, Littleman, Michael McGuiness, Oisín, Gerald Scarfe, David Simonds, Adam Singleton, Geoff Thompson, Martyn Turner and Richard Willson.

The author has made every effort to obtain permission to reproduce copyright material throughout the book. If any proper acknowledgement has not been made or permission not received, we would be grateful to be notified of any corrections that should be incorporated in the next edition or reprint of this volume.

Most of the cartoons have beeen reproduced from contemporary prints and newspapers, the print quality of which was occasionally poor. The author apologises for these imperfections and hopes they will not mar the reader's enjoyment and appreciation of the book.

OVERVIEW

Ulster has always been a unique and distinct province of Ireland. From the Red Branch Knights to the present day, there has been an otherness to the region and its people that has mystified strangers and created difficulties in Ulster's political and social relationships with its neighbours. The desire, indeed the necessity, to understand the Ulster people has been a motivating force for the rulers of these islands for more than nine centuries; and the depiction of the Ulster people to themselves and their neighbours has been central to that attempt at understanding. The ability to present the Ulster people pictorially greatly facilitated this process.

Printed representations of the natives of Ulster go back as far as the sixteenth century, and in manuscript form, further back still. Drawn by English commentators and aimed at an English audience, these early representations are mostly colonial stereotypes, depicting a wild and savage people who are to be feared and distrusted. John Derricke's *The Image of Irelande*, 'a notable discovery most lively describing the state of the wilde men of Ireland, properly called wood karne, with their actions and exercises, wherein they are daily occupied . . .', published in 1581, is a case in point. Derricke's book contains numerous plates illustrating the habits of the Ulster natives, the forces and strength of the English Crown, and the submission of the Great O'Neill, the Ulster lord who acknowledged and upheld the authority of Henry IV. The plate on page 2 shows an Irish Lord and his followers feasting. In multisequence, it depicts the killing and cooking of the calf, the blessing of the food, and the performances of the harper and the bard. To the extreme right, two men in wood kerne dress are pulling down their trousers and are about to defecate.

'An Irish Lord Feasting in the Open Air',
Derricke, *The Image of Irelande*, London, 1581

The words coming from the mouths of the two defecators read:

> Aspice spectator sic me docuere parentes
> See, beholder, this is how my parents taught me
>
> Me quoque maiores omnes virtute carentes
> All my worthless ancestors taught me that way too

In 1641, less than a century later, news of the Irish rebellion in the north of Ireland reached the parliament at Westminster via a deluge of 'authentic accounts', 'true histories' and 'melancholy addresses'. *The Last and Best Newes from Ireland*, for example, first published in London in 1641, detailed 'the warlike and cruell proceedures of the Rebels who are all papists and Jesuits of that Kingdome'. The events of 1641 were also amply represented in illustrations, such as John Temple's woodcut of friars watching drownings.

Unititled, *The Irish Rebellion*,
Temple, London, 1646

A century and a half later the cartoonist, an increasingly popular and influential social commentator, was provided with a rich source of material in the politics of the dis-United Kingdom of England, Scotland, Wales and Ireland. The growth of republicanism throughout Great Britain saw a number of attacks on King George III in the streets of London. James Gillray and others produced popular and telling images of such unrest.

'The Republican Attack', Gillray, London, 1795

The Society of United Irishmen, a radical, republican organisation dedicated to securing an independent Ireland, was founded in Belfast in 1791, and one of its most ardent proponents was a Cork man, Thomas Russell, who became librarian of the Belfast Society for Promoting Knowledge. Mary Ann McCracken, a devoted friend and supporter of the United Irishmen, described him as

a model of manly beauty, he was one of those favoured individuals whom one cannot pass in the street without being guilty of the rudeness of staring in the face while passing, and turning round to look at the receding figure. Though over six feet high, his majestic stature was scarcely observed owing to the exquisite symmetry of his form. Martial in his gait and demeanour . . . [with] dark and steady eye [and] compressed lip . . .

This nineteenth-century cartoonist presents him in caricature.

Above:
'Thomas Russell', Huffam,
Hibernian Magazine, Dublin, 1803

Right:
'The Librarian at Belfast', Linen Hall
Library, Belfast, *c.* 1794

In the early nineteenth century politics again provided material for humorous illustration. The 1830 election for the county of Down between Arthur Hill, Mathew Forde and Lord Castlereagh afforded this cartoonist scope for his art. The result was never in doubt with the established aristocratic Lords Castlereagh and Hill completely routing the candidate of the independent electors of the county, Colonel Mathew Forde.

'Hau'd your grip . . .', *Narrative of the Proceedings of the Contested Election for the County of Down, in the Year 1830*, Belfast, 1830

'Ireland a Nation – The Cabinet Council', Belfast, 1892

Later in the century sectarian conflict between Catholic and Protestant, unionist and nationalist, dominated affairs in Ulster. The differences between these groups became focused in the home rule crises of the 1880s and 1890s, setting the scene for the internecine warfare, both political and actual, of the twentieth century.

THE FOUNDATION
OF THE STATE

The state of Northern Ireland was established by the Government of Ireland Act in December 1920 and made up of six of the nine counties of Ulster. At the same time, and under the same Act, the state of Southern Ireland was established, comprising twenty-six counties: the three remaining counties of Ulster, and the provinces of Leinster, Munster and Connacht. The legislation was designed to acknowledge that a majority of people in the north of Ireland were intrinsically different from the rest of Ireland and wished to be part of the political entity known as the United Kingdom. This sense of difference was (and remains) rooted in the religion, culture and politics of the majority of people in the northern state: a people conscious of their history as planters, as practitioners of a truer religion than their neighbours, and as possessors of a sterner and more successful work ethic. It was not by chance that Ulster formed the focus of hostility to home rule in the 1880s and 1890s. In the face of Liberal leader William Gladstone's determination to give Ireland home rule, Lord Randolph Churchill decided to play the 'Orange card', a tactic designed to exploit Protestant fears of their

Catholic neighbours. On his arrival at Larne, County Antrim, in February 1886, he gave Ulster unionism the slogan that became its watchword – 'Ulster will fight and Ulster will be right'. The twentieth century in Ulster saw no end to the antipathy between Catholic and Protestant. Each week at the Custom House steps in Belfast, orators regaled an eager audience with the iniquities of the Pope of Rome and of the Roman Catholic Church. Such religious insights inevitably led to violence and to heightened sectarian tensions.

BELFAST SIGHTS for the British Association, 1902.

'Belfast Sights for the British Association, 1902',
Matt, *Nomad's Weekly*, Belfast,

Belfast Through English Eyes

'Belfast Through English Eyes', *Belfast Critic*, Belfast, 3 August 1901

During such confrontations the police kept a wary distance, unless hostilities were at such a pitch that intervention was unavoidable. The citizenry of Belfast, and a bemused British public, became so accustomed to this cavalier attitude to civil disturbance that the name of the police force, the Royal Irish Constabulary (RIC) – Royal since 1867 as a reward for suppressing the Fenian rising of that year – became a by-word for inactivity and indifference.

'Perjury . . . Brutality . . . Public Opinion . . . Neeson',
Matt, *Nomad's Weekly*, Belfast, 4 August 1900

The RIC was also a by-word for flagrant sectarian injustice. The case of Catholic workingman, Daniel Neeson, for example, outraged nationalists and unionists alike. Reacting to sectarian rioting in the Cullingtree Road area of Belfast in June 1900, police officers broke into the home of Neeson, a middle-aged Catholic man, and beat him in front of his family, seriously injuring him. Neeson was charged with rioting, and perjured police testimony was given against him. At the assizes Neeson was cleared of all charges against him but, because of his injuries, lost his job and was unable to support his family. The police officers involved in Neeson's assault and arrest were transferred from Belfast to other areas in the north of Ireland, not as a punishment, but because, as *Nomad's Weekly* reported, they 'had come into collision with the public'. Daniel Neeson received £25 in compensation, and there the matter came to an unsatisfactory conclusion.

'The Latest Job', Matt, *Nomad's Weekly*, Belfast, 11 August 1900

At City Hall the (generally) unstated, but universally understood, policy of jobs for the boys prevailed. As in other municipalities (both earlier and later), rewarding one's own might not be fair but it did make political sense. In Belfast there was the added benefit of being able to reward one's political supporter and religious brother at the same time.

11

WHICH WILL IT BE?

[It is now certain that a new form of government for Ireland will be laid bare within the next few months.]

Mr. Campbell-Bannerman conceals the pea in the old game of political thimble-rigging.

'Which Will It Be?', Matt, *Nomad's Weekly*, Belfast, 15 September 1906

Against this backdrop the debate about how Ireland (and Ulster) was to be governed raged on. The Irish Parliamentary Party, split by Charles Stewart Parnell's downfall in 1891, reunited under John Redmond in 1900 and began to lobby for a separate parliament for Ireland. Redmond knew that his best chance of success was to wait for the election of a Liberal government, where his party might hold the balance of power in a weak administration. This seemed a distinct possibility when, in 1906, the Liberal leader, Sir Henry Campbell-Bannerman, was elected prime minister.

Campbell-Bannerman toyed with ideas of home rule and devolution, but came to no decisive political conclusion. His willingness to consider the topic at all, however, raised the hopes and fears of the different political groupings in Ireland. In particular, it served to entrench the opposition of a small but growing number of northern unionists. No one at the time could foresee the consequences that would result from these political developments.

'The Stranger in the House',
S. MacM, *Republic*, Belfast,
27 December 1906

As the first decade of the twentieth century unfolded a Celtic Revival gripped Ireland and inspired a small group of young Ulster men and women to propound a spirited case for national self-determination for Ireland. In 1906 and 1907 the group published a radical political newspaper in Belfast which was dedicated to creating a separatist climate in Ireland, and to fostering the political ideals of the newly formed Sinn Féin movement. The name of their newspaper was the *Republic*, a title little calculated to endear it to the majority of people in Ulster. Their message was simple, immediate and revolutionary, and their newspaper was quickly banned.

If the authorities in Ulster and Belfast were not prepared for such a revolutionary political philosophy, neither were they receptive to Labour politics. When James Larkin's National Union of Dock Labourers went on strike in 1907 for better pay and conditions, their Belfast employers brought in strike breakers from Liverpool, Hull and Glasgow. There followed violent clashes between strikers and blackleg labourers and carters who were engaged to ferry coal and produce from the docks.

'A Waring St Incident', *Irish Independent*, Dublin, 5 August 1907

PUNCTURED!

'Punctured', *Northern Star*, Belfast, 10 August 1907

Members of the RIC who were engaged to protect the wares of the shipping magnates and merchants of Belfast felt some sympathy for the striking men and their families. Constable William Barrett, for example, refused to give protection to the strike-breaking driver of a motor wagon laden with goods, and precipitated a short-lived police strike in sympathy with the dock labourers. Such a serious mutiny could only have one outcome, and Barrett was dismissed from the service, while other police strikers were transferred to posts outside Belfast.

KICKED

"Say Au-Revoir, but not good-bye!" After his strenuous protestations that HE would never submit to the policy of the "OPEN SHOP", i.e., that Trades Unionists should work beside Non-Unionists, Lanky Larkin has made his exit from Belfast.

'Kicked', Matt, *Nomad's Weekly*, Belfast, 24 August 1907

The dockers' strike was broken, and the strikers were offered even worse terms if they wished to return to work. Larkin, originally from Liverpool, left Belfast, taking with him valuable lessons that he would later use in similar confrontations in Dublin and America.

16

After the death of Campbell-Bannerman in 1908 Herbert H. Asquith (below left) became prime minister. He was much more receptive to the idea of home rule and Redmond (below right), seeing his chance, used all his political acumen and charm to advance the cause of home rule.

'The Beauties of Home Rule', London, n.d.

THE FIGHT THAT CAN'T BE STOPPED.

THE NORTH TYRONE CHAMPIONSHIP between E. C. Herdman (Loyalist) and
T. W. Russell (Disruptionist), to be fought To-morrow (Friday, 6th October).

'The Fight That Can't Be Stopped', Greer, *Nomad's Weekly*, Belfast, 7 October 1911

Unionist leader Edward Carson, sitting in the loyalist corner, was emerging
as a powerful and influential figure in the fight against home rulers. In the
opposing corner, upholding the cause of Catholic nationalism, is Cardinal
Michael Logue, archbishop of Armagh.

'The Latest Liberal Lay', Lemon, *Town Topics*, Belfast, 12 April 1912

As the debate on home rule hotted up, so too did opposition in Ulster. In 1911 the Ulster Women's Unionist Council was formed to help maintain the union between Great Britain and Ireland. In the same year, Carson spelled out his implacable opposition to home rule in an address to fifty thousand members of the Orange Order and Unionist Clubs at Craigavon, the home of Captain James Craig. This increase in unionist activity was due to Asquith's now open commitment to home rule which he had given in return for Redmond's support in the House of Commons. Unionist fears were heightened again in August 1911 when the Parliament Act withdrew the veto power of the House of Lords, thereby taking away the safeguard of a Lords' veto to any home rule bill. Such fears were, in fact, well-founded: in April 1912, Asquith, still dependent on Redmond's Irish Parliamentary Party to hold a majority in the Commons, was prevailed upon to introduce the Home Rule Bill.

'We Hereby . . .', Morrow,
Graphic, London,
28 September 1912

Unionist reaction to the Bill was swift, well-organised and implacable. A unionist demonstration in the Albert Hall in London in June was followed by a highly successful set piece involving the signing of the Solemn League and Covenant in Belfast on 28 September 1912.

To-day (Saturday) witnesses the culminating act of the fierce political campaign in Ulster against Home Rule, the signing of the Solemn Covenant of resistance throughout the North of Ireland. Ten strenuous days of fiery oratory and continuous public demonstrations, under the personal leadership of Sir Edward Carson, have stirred all classes in town and country to a pitch of fierce excitement unknown in Ireland since the Battle of the Boyne, over two hundred years ago.

'The Orange Drums', Morrow, *Graphic*, London, 28 September 1912

"I promise you that so long as you stand firm I and those associated with me will *most certainly* stand firm, and we never will have Home Rule."

Sir Edward Carson addressing the Belfast Division of the Ulster Volunteer Force at Belfast, 27th September, 1913.

'Ulster at Bay', Greer, *Nomad's Weekly*, Belfast, 5 October 1913

In January 1913 Edward Carson's proposed amendment to the Home Rule Bill, which argued for the exclusion of the nine counties of Ulster from home rule, was defeated and the Bill passed its third Commons reading. Since political means had failed to halt home rule, unionists decided that other means must now be tried. Within the month the Ulster Volunteer Force (represented below by Carson) was formed with the sworn aim of defeating home rule (represented below by Redmond), by physical force if necessary.

21

"THERE'S MANY A SLIP . . ."

IN April, 1914, the Home Rule Bill offered to Mr. REDMOND by Mr. ASQUITH, with safeguards for Ulster, was rejected by CARSON and wrecked by the action of the Generals at the Curragh, who resigned rather than run the risk of fighting against Ulster. A conference summoned by the KING failed on the eve of the War, and the Bill was indefinitely postponed.

'There's Many a Slip . . .', Partridge, *Punch*, London, 1 April 1914

In March 1914 rumours that the UVF were about to raid arms depots in Ulster led the British government to take military precautions. However, under the leadership of General Hubert Gough, fifty-eight officers at the Curragh army camp in County Kildare threatened to resign their commissions if they were ordered to take up arms against Ulster unionists. Negotiations defused the situation, but the reality of armed rebellion was recognised.

This reality was given fresh impetus on the night of 24–25 April 1914, when at least twenty-five thousand rifles and three million rounds of ammunition were landed at Larne in County Antrim, and Donaghadee and Bangor on the County Down coast, and distributed throughout Ulster by the UVF.

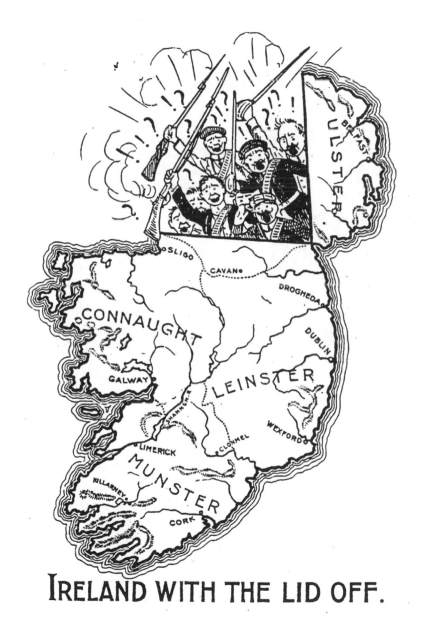

IRELAND WITH THE LID OFF.

'Ireland with the Lid Off', postcard, Linen Hall Library, Belfast, c. 1914

'Masonic Proclamation', postcard, Historic Events Series,
Linen Hall Library, Belfast, *c.* 1914

Unsuccessful attempts by the RIC to locate these arms caches pointed
towards open collusion with the UVF. This suspicion was reinforced in July
1914 when Erskine Childers landed fifteen hundred rifles and a large
amount of ammunition at Howth, County Dublin, for the Irish Volunteers.
On this occasion, government forces were quick to intervene, although only
after Irish Volunteers had paraded the rifles in the streets. Government
troops fired on the crowd who had gathered, killing four people and
wounding many others. The event served to increase nationalist suspicions
and resentment.

Events in the wider world, however, overtook the conflicts and disputes in Ireland. On 28 June the heir to the throne of the Austro-Hungarian Empire was assassinated in Sarajevo, setting into motion a chain of events that would lead to the First World War. Two months later Britain took up arms against Germany and the Home Rule Bill was suspended for the duration of the war. Both John Redmond and Edward Carson pledged the support of their followers to the war effort.

WONDERS WILL NEVER CEASE

'Wonders Will Never Cease', Walker, *Daily Graphic*, London, 1914

1916 Commemoration Souvenir　　　　*Padraig Pearse reads the Proclamation*

'Padraig Pearse Reads the Proclamation', commemorative postcard,
Linen Hall Library, Belfast, 1966

In spite of Redmond's promise a significant number of the Irish Volunteers,
under Eoin MacNeill, were resistant to the call for support for Great Britain,
and refused to go into battle unless Ireland was given independence. This
opposition was epitomised in the republican rebellion of Easter 1916,
carried out by the Irish Volunteers. The postcard above shows Padraig
Pearse, one of the leaders of the rebellion, reading the proclamation which
declared Ireland a republic. Within two weeks, however, the insurrection
had been quashed and Pearse, along with the other signatories of the
proclamation, had been executed.

'Charge of the Ulster Division', Conor, postcard, Linen Hall Library, Belfast, *c.* 1916

In July 1916, in an event which served to expose the enormity of the division in political opinion in Ireland, 5,500 men of the 36th (Ulster) Division were killed or wounded at the Battle of the Somme. Such a sacrifice was seen as a testament of the loyalty of the Protestants of Ulster, and compared starkly with the nationalist rebellion which had taken place only a few months earlier.

A FATEFUL SESSION.
SITTING HEN. "GO AWAY! DON'T HURRY ME!"

'A Fateful Session', Raven-Hill, *Punch*, London, 1 August 1917

In 1917 David Lloyd George, who had succeeded Asquith as prime minister the previous year, proposed that an Irish Convention be convened so that the Irish question could be resolved. The Convention met for its plenary session on 25 July 1917 under the chairmanship of Sir Horace Plunkett, the noted land reformer. Its deliberations lasted for the next nine months, by which time its belated recommendation for the establishment of a home rule parliament for the whole of Ireland was largely ignored by an exasperated public.

THE PHILANDERER.

Sinn Féin. "BE MINE."
President Wilson. "I DO HOPE I HAVEN'T GIVEN YOU TOO MUCH ENCOURAGEMENT
—BUT I CAN NEVER BE MORE THAN A BROTHER TO YOU."

'The Philanderer', Partridge, *Punch*, London, 25 June 1919

By 1918 a new nationalist coalition called Sinn Féin had been formed. Under the leadership of Eamon de Valera, it established itself as the leading nationalist party in the general election of December 1918, gaining seventy-three seats in contrast to the six seats won by the Irish Parliamentary Party. The Ulster unionists returned twenty-six members. In January 1919, Sinn Féin set up its own (unrecognised) Irish parliament, Dáil Éireann. Also in January 1919, the president of the United States of America, Woodrow Wilson, was granted the freedom of the city of Dublin. His Fourteen Points for postwar peace, which included the 'free, open-minded and impartial adjustment of colonial claims', encouraged Sinn Féin to demand national self-determination for the whole of Ireland, a demand that was rejected at Westminster.

THE KINDEST CUT OF ALL.

WELSH WIZARD. "I NOW PROCEED TO CUT THIS MAP INTO TWO PARTS AND PLACE THEM IN THE HAT. AFTER A SUITABLE INTERVAL THEY WILL BE FOUND TO HAVE COME TOGETHER OF THEIR OWN ACCORD—(*ASIDE*)—AT LEAST LET'S HOPE SO; I'VE NEVER DONE THIS TRICK BEFORE."

'The Kindest Cut of All', Partridge, *Punch*, London, 10 March 1920

In Ulster, Edward Carson was arguing the unionist case and deploying his troops to best advantage. Amid increasing violence in the south and west of Ireland, he endorsed Lloyd George's proposal for the exclusion of six of the nine Ulster counties from the home rule settlement for Ireland. The proposal was introduced into the House of Commons on 25 February 1920, and accepted by a majority of the Ulster Unionist Council on 10 March. Known as the Better Government of Ireland Act, it became law on 23 December 1920. Its creator, Lloyd George, knew that it might, indeed must, create as many problems as it might solve. For the present, however, it would suffice. Its terms allowed for the creation of the states of Northern Ireland and Southern Ireland, and also for a Council of Ireland which would seek to bring both states together under a single parliament.

A PROTESTANT PARLIAMENT FOR A PROTESTANT PEOPLE

In February 1921 Sir James Craig succeeded an increasingly weary and disillusioned Edward Carson as leader of the Ulster Unionists.

'Sir James Craig', Q.E.D.,
Ulster Opinion, Belfast, 8 March 1923

STARTING THE SETTLEMENT.

'Starting the Settlement', Raven-Hill, *Punch*, London, 8 June 1921

The first general election in Northern Ireland was held on 24 May 1921, and set a precedent in the United Kingdom by using proportional representation. The results of the election were predictable: forty seats for the Unionists, six for Sinn Féin and six for the Nationalist Party. In June, when the parliament of Northern Ireland met for the first time in Belfast City Hall, it was boycotted by Nationalists and Sinn Féin. George v, in Belfast for the opening ceremony, pleaded for reconciliation between the two communities in the new state.

The prime minister, Winston Churchill, had attempted to deal with the violence in 1920 with the formation of the Special Ulster Constabulary, which was made up entirely of Protestants and structurally modelled on the UVF. It was divided into three sections: the A Specials, who numbered 2,000 and who were full-time and salaried; the B Specials, who numbered 19,500 and who were part-time and unpaid; and the C Specials, an unpaid reserve force.

THE AMBUSH

An artist's impression of the ambush of the "A" Specials at the Six Towns

'The Ambush', McCullagh, *Guns in Ulster*, Belfast, 1967

34

'The Swatragh Ambush, June 1921', McCullagh, *Guns in Ulster*, Belfast, 1967

In November 1921 the government of Northern Ireland took over responsibility for law and order in the state. With the recently formed Ulster Special Constabulary and the soon to be designated Royal Ulster Constabulary, Craig set about securing the state and halting the border attacks orchestrated by IRA units operating on both sides of the border. Above is an ambush of RIC officers at Swatragh in County Londonderry in June 1921.

A FORGOTTEN PATRIOTISM.

SHADE OF PARNELL (*to Mr. DE VALERA*). "I SUPPOSE I LOVED MY COUNTRY AT LEAST AS WELL AS YOU DO; BUT I SHOULD HAVE BEEN SATISFIED WITH THE HALF OF THAT OFFER."

'A Forgotten Patriotism', *Punch*, London, 24 August 1921

In the south of Ireland de Valera categorically rejected the terms of the Act of 1920.

THE MAD BULL

FARMER CRAIG. "IF YOU CAN'T KEEP THAT BRUTE ON YOUR SIDE OF THE FENCE I
SHALL DEAL WITH HIM AS I THINK FIT."
FARMER COLLINS. "WELL BETWEEN YOU AND ME, I WISH TO GOD YE WOULD."

'The Mad Bull', Partridge, *Punch*, London, 15 February 1922

After some of the worst sectarian violence witnessed in Derry and Belfast, the British government and the IRA agreed a truce, taking effect from 11 July 1921. This opened the way for negotiations and in October Sir James Craig met with Michael Collins, commander in chief of the IRA, in London. On 6 December, Craig and Collins signed the Anglo-Irish Treaty, which conferred upon Southern Ireland the status of a dominion and renamed it the Irish Free State. The status of Northern Ireland was guaranteed and, in the event that it should continue as a separate state, a boundary commission was to be set up to decide the border between the two states. The agreement, which failed to secure the status of a republic for Ireland, created a major split among nationalists, and although it was ratified by the Dáil, it succeeded only by a small majority. Collins, seen by anti-treaty forces to have performed a betrayal in his signing of the agreement, was forced into conflict with former friends and allies, including those in the IRA.

THE NEW FORCE.

IRISH GUNMAN. "SAINTS PRESERVE US! AN INFERNAL MACHINE!"

[It is to be hoped that the authority conferred upon the Provisional Government by the voice of the people, as expressed in the recent Elections, may bring to an end the campaign of murder—culminating in the brutal assassination of Field-Marshal Sir HENRY WILSON—which has disgraced the name of Ireland in the eyes of the whole world.]

'The New Force', Partridge, *Punch*, London, 28 June 1922

The unstable nature of the new governments in Northern Ireland and the Irish Free State was exacerbated by on-going violence throughout large areas of the country. The tension between parliamentary politics and political terror was highlighted in June 1922 when Sir Henry Wilson, military adviser to the government of Northern Ireland, was murdered by the IRA in London.

In 1924, when the question of the Boundary Commission was raised under the terms of the 1921 Treaty, Sir James Craig formally declined to nominate a representative from Northern Ireland. Justice Richard Feetham of the South African Supreme Court was Westminster's representative and chairman, Eoin MacNeill represented the Free State and, in the end, Westminster appointed J.R. Fisher as the Northern Ireland commissioner. The commission proceeded to take soundings on both sides of the existing border, but the exercise was little more than a costly farce. The tripartite agreement between Northern Ireland, the Free State and Great Britain concluded by recognising the existing border.

THE BOUNDARY LINE.

'The Boundary Line', Alpha, *Ulster Review*, Belfast, June 1924

UNITED IRELAND.

The Government of the Irish Free State has accepted the existing boundary-line, on condition of being absolved from their responsibility for a portion of the National Debt. It is understood that the Government of Northern Ireland will also reap some financial compensation for non-disturbance.

'United Ireland', *Punch*, London, 9 December 1925

In return for agreeing to the existing boundary, the southern government was absolved from its proportion of the British national debt. Northern Ireland also received a beneficial financial settlement. As the cartoon above shows – John Bull (centre) is having his pocket picked by the leader of the Northern Irish state, James Craig (right) and the leader of the Irish Free State, T.W. Cosgrave (left) – the partition of Ireland was achieved at a high cost to the British taxpayer.

In May 1927 James Craig was created Viscount Craigavon of Stormont, and settled down to maintaining unionist domination of the Northern Ireland state. In April 1929, he abolished proportional representation in Northern Ireland elections, a political manoeuvre which, along with redrawing of the electoral boundaries, was designed to increase the unionist majority and to split the Labour and Nationalist vote. The move was a successful one and in the general election of May 1929 Nationalists lost one seat and Labour lost two. The Unionist majority, which had dropped to 36 in the 1925 election, was increased to 40. The Nationalists were led by Joseph Devlin, who orchestrated a spirited, if ultimately unsuccessful, opposition to the policies of the unionist majority.

Craig versus Devlin
The everlasting round Contest – Bigotry rather than Commonsense

'Craig Versus Devlin', *Belfast Topics*, Belfast, May 1927

Around the same time a new parliament building was being erected at Stormont, on Belfast's Upper Newtownards Road. On 30 September 1932, the last sitting of the parliament of Northern Ireland in Belfast City Hall took place against a backdrop of civil unrest and destitution among a large section of the urban unemployed. Jack Beattie, Labour MP for Pottinger, distinguished himself by throwing the mace on the floor in protest at the government's apathy in the face of widespread social need. For a brief moment in Ulster's history Protestant and Catholic unemployed came together in a series of strikes and demonstrations to protest at their lot. Baton charges by the RUC and curfews were the government's answer to the situation, as well as a ban on marches under the Special Powers Act. Outdoor relief was increased but the ban on marches was upheld for the sake of public order.

IN THE CAUSE OF MUSIC

'In the Cause of Music', *PTQ*, Belfast, 1936

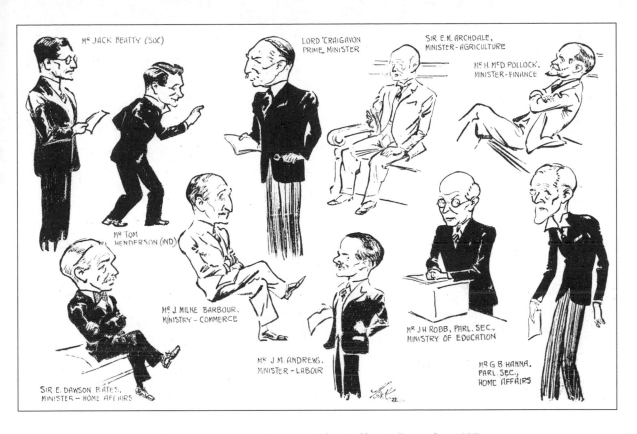

'Parliamentarians', *Northern Whig*, Belfast, 1 December 1937

The new home of the parliament of Northern Ireland at Stormont was opened by the Prince of Wales on 16 November 1932, with great ceremony. It epitomised to the unionist hegemony their maturity, solidity and dignity as a state. To the nationalists of Northern Ireland it was, and would continue to be, a symbol of their exclusion from political power. The attitude of the unionist community to the Catholic and nationalist minority was summed up in a remark made by Sir James Craig at a Twelfth of July parade in 1932, when he told the assembled people, 'Ours is a Protestant government and I am an Orangeman.' The following year, John Andrews, MP for Mid-Down and prime minister of Northern Ireland between 1940 and 1943, refuted a scurrilous allegation made against his government that it was soft on the minority. He said, 'Another allegation made against the Government, which is untrue, is that out of thirty-one porters at Stormont, twenty-eight are Roman Catholics. I have investigated the matter and I have found that there are thirty Protestants and only one Roman Catholic, there only temporarily . . .' In the same year Craig told the Northern House of Commons: 'All I boast is that we are a Protestant Parliament and a Protestant State.'

'A White Horse . . .', *PTQ*, Belfast, 1936

Nationalist reaction to such blatant abuses of political power was necessarily muted. Satire, however, did provide some outlet for nationalist grievances. Here, the regal proportions and sumptuous furnishings of Stormont, created to house the parliament of one of the smallest countries in the world, are under attack.

THE BALLYNAHINCH WAR MEMORIAL.

A short time ago an ancient inhabitant of Ballynahinch awoke one morning to realise to his horror that the town was without a War Memorial. He called a public meeting forthwith, at which it was decided to make good the deficiency, and to raise funds the Civil Service Choir was invited to give a Concert. As no particular war was mentioned, the exact form the Memorial should take was the subject of acute controversy. Some suggested a village pump suitably inscribed, whilst others favoured restorations to a certain religious edifice in the district.

To help the town out of its difficulty, the Stormont Revue artist produced the design shown above. We are happy to say it met with universal approval.

'The Ballynahinch War Memorial', *Stormont Review*, Belfast, March 1933

The grandeur of such trappings contrasted with the reality of governing a small population and geographical area. Affairs of state often gave way to the minutiae of local government. In 1933, for example, the inhabitants of the market town of Ballynahinch, in the centre of County Down, were keen to erect a war memorial to commemorate those who had fallen in the First World War. The sectarian and cultural divisions of society in Northern Ireland are exemplified in this satirical suggestion for a fitting memorial which appeared in a civil service magazine.

In the mid-1930s two of Northern Ireland's most charismatic political leaders died. In January 1934, Joseph Devlin, president of the Ancient Order of Hibernians, MP for Fermanagh and Tyrone at Westminster and leader of the opposition at Stormont, passed away. He was profoundly mourned by the nationalist constituency in the North.

ENGLAND *v.* IRISH FREE STATE.
Umpire: MR. DEVLIN.

'England v. Irish Free State', A.W.L., *Punch*, London, 13 July 1932

A year later, Sir Edward Carson died at his home in England. He had been deeply moved, two years earlier, at the unveiling of the Carson monument at Stormont, on the base of which was the inscription, 'Erected by the loyalists of Ulster as an expression of their love and admiration for the Rt Hon. F.E. Lord Carson of Duncairn'.

'Lord Carson of Duncairn', Q.E.D., *Ulster Opinion*, Belfast, 2 March 1923

The world was changing rapidly and, in the latter part of the 1930s, a second European war loomed. Mussolini, Hitler, de Valera, Craig and many others had to decide on their roles in that conflict.

SILLIEST SYMPHONY

'Silliest Symphony', Nisbet, *PTQ*, Belfast, 1935

'The Battle of York Street, 1990', *PTQ*, Belfast, 1936

In spite of the impending war, certain things within Northern Ireland did not change. In 1936, following sectarian rioting in Belfast the previous year, in which York Street had been a flashpoint, *PTQ*, the Queen's Students' Union magazine, cast an eye forward half a century and envisioned life in Belfast in 1990. The artist has succeeded in producing an uncannily accurate view of community relations in the future.

"SUNDAY MUSIC IN THE PARKS."

PERSECUTOR: "Your worship, the Prisoner (Mr. Bird) is charged with creating Music in the Parks on Sunday (cries of horror). He has outraged our principles and has committed a most heinous crime. I demand his extermination."

'Sunday Music in the Parks', Ramsbottom, *Northern Light*, Belfast, May 1938

Keeping the Sabbath holy also continued to exercise the minds of church and state in Northern Ireland . . .

. . . And the machinations of their nearest neighbours were always to be feared.

'A Prominent Dublin Mathematician . . .', *PTQ*, Belfast, 1936

But the inevitable conflict, occasioned by Hitler's ambitions in Europe, could not be avoided or deflected. The Spanish Civil War of 1936 was a forerunner of the more global warfare to follow, and Irishmen, North and South, fought and died in Spain as governments in these islands debated their position in the coming conflict.

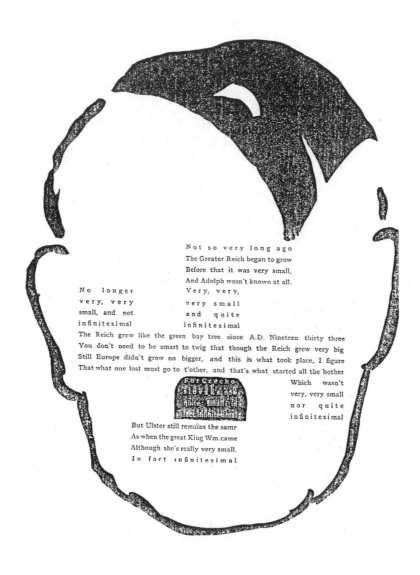

Not so very long ago
The Greater Reich began to grow
Before that it was very small,
And Adolph wasn't known at all.
Very, very,
very small
and quite
infinitesimal

No longer
very, very
small, and not
infinitesimal

The Reich grew like the green bay tree since A.D. Nineteen thirty three
You don't need to be smart to twig that though the Reich grew very big
Still Europe didn't grow no bigger, and this is what took place, I figure
That what one lost must go to t'other, and that's what started all the bother

Which wasn't
very, very small
nor quite
infinitesimal

For Czecho-
slovakia now
quite small in
fact infinitesimal

But Ulster still remains the same
As when the great Kiug Wm. came
Although she's really very small,
In fact infinitesimal

'Hitler', PTQ, Belfast, 1939

When war was declared between Great Britain and Germany on 3 September 1939, Lord Craigavon, prime minister of Northern Ireland, pledged the fighting might of Ulster to the British war effort.

Undefeated Champion
of the
British Empire
1922–1938

'Undefeated Champion of the British Empire 1922–1938',
Stewart, *PTQ*, Belfast, 1938

ULSTER AT WAR

On 22 December 1938, the government of Northern Ireland reintroduced internment without trial under the Special Powers Act. Police intelligence had uncovered plans for an IRA campaign against the northern state and against England in this period of international tension. Within a month the IRA army council had issued an ultimatum calling for British troops to be withdrawn from Northern Ireland or face reprisals. In the greater European crisis unfolding in the early months of 1939, such an ultimatum was noted, but the ramifications of an all-out war against Germany dominated the concerns of government in London and at Stormont.

'In the Balance', Conn, *Dublin Opinion*, Dublin, January 1939

The probability of air raids against strategic targets in Great Britain and Northern Ireland was given much thought by the Home Office, who drew up guidelines for effective protection against such an eventuality. Householders were told how to protect their homes and how to choose and reinforce a refuge room. They were encouraged to stockpile candles and matches and other essentials, to observe the blackout regulations, and to make their refuge impervious to gas. But the reality of the air raids, when they came, shocked the populace.

'Oh, Daddy – Look What I Found!', Gianni, *PTQ*, Belfast, 1941

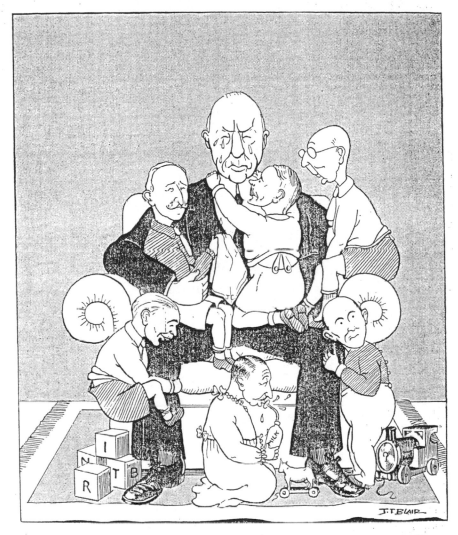

" Cheer Up Uncle Jimmy, You Always Have Us."

'No Conscription for Northern Ireland', Blair, *PTQ*, Belfast, 1940

On 15 March 1939, German troops entered Prague, the capital of Czechoslovakia, as conquerors. War was inevitable and, on 27 April 1939, the British government introduced conscription of men aged between twenty and twenty-one years of age. Protests in the North and in the Free State persuaded the British government not to apply conscription to Northern Ireland. The picture above shows a disappointed Sir James Craig being comforted by his cabinet, including Sir Basil Brooke (forefront), destined to be the third prime minister of Northern Ireland.

"Now who's that shouting 'Spray'?
— oh, it's all right; it isn't one
of our fellows!"

**Well, do _you_ know _exactly_ what to do _immediately_
you hear anyone shout 'Spray'?**

'Well, do you know exactly what to do?', poster,
Linen Hall Library, Belfast, *c.* 1939

The prime minister of Northern Ireland, Lord Craigavon, pledged the complete integration of the resources of Northern Ireland into the war effort. In a speech at Stormont on 4 September 1939, he told a hushed chamber:

> We here are today in a state of war and we are prepared with the rest of the United Kingdom to face all the responsibilities that this imposes on the people of Ulster. There is no slackening of our

loyalty. There is no falling off in our determination to place the whole of our resources at the disposal of the Government in Britain . . .

Northern Ireland now began to prepare for war in earnest. All centrally printed manuals for civil defence were distributed widely amongst the population. Industry and agriculture were put on a war footing, with ever increased and more cost-effective output the aim. Basic training in air-raid precautions was given throughout the north of Ireland, in schools and in church halls. A poster campaign on this and other aspects of life in wartime was launched. Some of the information was basic commonsense. In the event of mustard gas or other poisonous gas being sprayed from enemy aircraft the advice was as follows: 'The risk to persons in the open will be obvious, but the danger may be avoided by remaining under cover.'

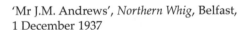

MR J.M. ANDREWS.
MINISTER - LABOUR.

'Mr J.M. Andrews', *Northern Whig*, Belfast, 1 December 1937

But it was in England that the first air raids came. On 7 September 1940, the Battle of Britain began. The German Luftwaffe attacked Woolwich arsenal, a power station, a gas works, the docks and the City of London. The targets were obvious – industry and the civilian population. Belfast, with its strategic importance to Britain's North Atlantic seaway, and its growing weapons production capability, braced itself for the onslaught from the air. As Northern Ireland was about to suffer its most damaging experience of the war, its first prime minister, the ageing and increasingly frail Viscount Craigavon, retired. John Andrews took his place as prime minister and leader of the Unionist Party.

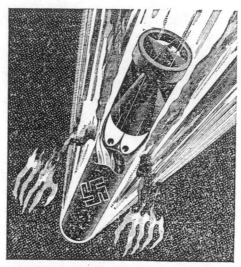

FIREBOMB FRITZ
will come again —
Are you ready
to put him out?

YES! Britain's Fire Guard — we men and women of Britain — are resolved and ready to save our factories, our railways, our food, our homes. Fire Guard work is often dull, sometimes dangerous, but it's a job that's got to be done. Our heart and soul is in it. We train and we practise. We know our sectors like the backs of our hands — every corner, every roof top. We watch. We climb ladders, work pumps, wield sandbags. We will shatter Firebomb Fritz and all the Nazi horrors he stands for.

FIRE GUARD TIPS
No. 1.

Firebombs that fall in the street are usually harmless unless they are close to something inflammable, like a motor vehicle. Look for bombs on buildings first.

BRITAIN
SHALL NOT
BURN!

ISSUED BY THE MINISTRY OF PUBLIC SECURITY

'Firebomb Fritz . . .', *Belfast News-Letter*, Belfast, 10 September 1941

On the night of 7–8 April 1941, the first Luftwaffe attacks on the city of Belfast began: thirteen people were killed. A week later nearly 300 German bombs rained down on Belfast, killing an estimated 900 people and injuring 1,500. In early May the planes returned, this time targeting the shipyards, Shorts' aircraft factory, the harbour power station and York Street railway station. One hundred and fifty people were killed and as many seriously injured.

At the time it was alleged that the route to Belfast had been lit from Dublin by anti-partitionists.

Another Northern Ireland Black-Out Problem Overcome

'Another Northern Ireland Black-out Problem Overcome',
Maskee, *Dublin Opinion*, Dublin, February 1940

"Never mind about it not being 'arf wot we're giving them—let's git 'ome."

'Never mind about it not being . . .',
Giles, *Sunday Express*, London, 27 February 1944

The spirit of resistance to such bombings, and the determination of the people of Northern Ireland was bolstered by that of the population of London who experienced even greater devastation.

A home guard, based on the English Local Defence Volunteers, was set up in Northern Ireland from early 1941. The 'Dad's Army' image of some of the early English units was countered in Northern Ireland by basing the units on existing Ulster Special Constabulary units, and providing distinctive uniforms from the outset. In the absence of an existing territorial force, Local Defence Volunteers undertook security duties, guarding key installations and releasing regular units for more essential duties. Using their local knowledge to good effect, they were instrumental in frustrating the activities of the IRA, who sought to make common cause with Germany against Great Britain.

'Derry . . . Tyrone . . . Fermanagh . . .',
Traill, *1st Derry City Battalion: Ulster Home Guard*, Souvenir Review, Belfast, 1944

As the war in Europe and Africa progressed, and German victory followed German victory, the United States of America began to review its position of neutrality. In April 1941 US troops occupied Greenland to protect the North Atlantic trade route between America and Great Britain. In August, President Franklin D. Roosevelt and Prime Minister Winston Churchill agreed the Atlantic Charter which set out the joint war and peace aims of the two nations. When the USS *Reuben James*, on convoy duty in the North Atlantic, was sunk by German U-boats, the United States took one step closer to joining the war. The surprise attack on Pearl Harbor on 7 December 1941 was the event that finally led them to join the Allies. Once committed, they moved swiftly. On 26 January 1942, the first American troops arrived in Ulster, and quickly established themselves in bases throughout the country.

Howard E. M'Claren
(Michigan)

G Campbell

Bob Lougee
(Maine)

Katzner Irving
(New Jersey)

'GIS', Campbell, *Ulster in Black and White*, Belfast, 1945

The War and Navy Departments in Washington DC thought it prudent to provide their servicemen with a factual guide to their new billets. They issued *A Pocket Guide to Northern Ireland* in which they explained the weather and the language:

> [Northern Ireland] is a small country, only slightly bigger than the State of Connecticut . . . First off you may not like the Irish climate. It is damp, chilly, rainy . . . The sun is only an occasional visitor in Ireland . . .
>
> The Ulster accent may at first be hard to understand . . . Many of the expressions may strike you as funny; some of them may not be understandable . . . [You should know] that a drug store is a chemist's shop; that garters are 'sock suspenders' and . . . that a streetcar is a 'tram' . . .

" I wanna get me a street car "

'I wanna get me a street car', Campbell, *Ulster in Black and White*, Belfast, 1945

Another important piece of information for the American serviceman was how to conduct oneself in the 'male social centre in Ulster . . . the tavern or public house'. The advice was practical and to the point:

Most people [in Northern Ireland] drink stout, ale, and porter, which they call beer. Up in the hills you may be offered an illicit concoction called 'potheen' . . . Watch it. It's dynamite. The Irish don't go in for the Dutch treat system. If five men enter a pub, each will stand a round, and etiquette demands that all stay until the last of the five rounds has been bought. If you are invited to join such a group, and do so, remember that you will give offence by a refusal to treat and be treated . . . The Irish love to talk . . . Argument for its own sake is a Scotch-Irish specialty, and arguing politics might almost be called a national sport. The pub is the principal forum . . . In Ulster it is quite within the rules of the game to accuse your adversary not only of pig stealing, but of actual treason. A word of warning: your place in these arguments is on the side-lines.

Little wonder then that many American servicemen felt it was safer to fraternise with their own kind.

Untitled, Campbell, *Ulster in Black and White*, Belfast, 1945

American Ways

'American Ways', Campbell, *Ulster in Black and White*, Belfast, 1945

If they felt safer drinking with their own, these young American men were keen to meet women in Northern Ireland. How should they be approached? Once again, the guide was invaluable:

> Irish girls are friendly. They will stop on the country road and pass the time of day. Don't think on that account that they are falling for you in a big way. If you're interested in dancing, you'll find partners without difficulty in Belfast and the other big towns. You'll hear American popular songs . . . but in the country, dances are . . . rare and the jive is unknown . . . One point: cutting in is frowned upon. Watch the other men and follow their example . . .

Despite the necessity of remembering a complicated set of social rules, many GIs met their future wives in the dance halls of Northern Ireland. A companion guide, explaining contemporary America, might have been a boon for Northern Irish brides.

"But honey—where did you get the idea that all Americans live in skyscrapers?"
(*Acknowledgments to Paul Webb*)

'But honey . . .', Giles, *Sunday Express*, London, 3 February 1946

When the war ended in 1945, Churchill, in a letter to John Andrews, was moved to praise Northern Ireland's contribution to the eventual victory of the Allies, and to point out that 'but for the loyalty of Northern Ireland and its devotion . . . the light which now shines so strongly throughout the world would have been quenched . . .' As a vital part of the war effort, building ships and tanks and making munitions, Northern Ireland had demonstrated once again its loyalty and commitment to Britain. Any fear that its indigenous culture had been perverted by exposure to outside influences was unfounded . . .

" MA ! WHO'S THE COWBOY ? "

'Ma! Who's the Cowboy?', McG and King, *PTQ*, Belfast, 1945

Schwartz Over Ulster!

'Schwartz Over Ulster!', Friers, *PTQ*, Belfast, 1940

The war effort in Northern Ireland was concentrated in two particular areas. On the war front, Northern Ireland provided a base for allied training and manufactured essential munitions. On the home front, maintaining and strengthening the constitutional position of Northern Ireland within the Empire was a major priority. Vigilance against the IRA, who were suspected of having links with Hitler, was acute, and all internal IRA activity and collaboration was monitored and thwarted.

Nationalists in Northern Irleland were little encouraged, even had they been inclined, to join the war effort. The home guard, recruited from the ranks of the Special Constabulary, was an unwelcoming organisation, while employment in the shipyards and munitions factories invariably went to supporters of the Northern Ireland government. The only peaceful means of lodging objection to this state of affairs was through the pages of fringe, and therefore little heeded, publications.

'Believe it or Not', *PTQ*, Belfast, 1940

SECRET POLICE OF THE NATIONS 1

SECRET POLICE OF THE NATIONS 2

SECRET POLICE OF THE NATIONS 3

GESTAPO (GERMANY)

OVRA (ITALY)

OGPU (RUSSIA)

SECRET POLICE OF THE NATIONS 4

B–SPECIALS (ULSTER)

'Secret Police of the Nations', Friers, *PTQ*, Belfast, 1940

The predominantly Protestant police force, and the exclusively Protestant Special Constabulary, were the pride of the unionist community, and a bastion against integration into an all-Ireland and Catholic republic. For the Catholic and nationalist community, however, the police were a source of fear and resentment.

Throughout the war years, there were two political realities that angered and frustrated the unionist majority in Northern Ireland. The first was the neutrality of the Irish Free State. Ireland's neutrality in the war was universally condemned by unionists in the North. In his victory speech of May 1945, Churchill singled out Taoiseach Eamon de Valera for specific and particular attack in this regard. De Valera responded that Éire could not in all conscience join in a grand alliance with the country which had engineered its partition.

'That Was An Taoiseach', CEK, *Dublin Opinion*, Dublin, June 1945

The second was the growth of cross-border black-market trade in scarce and rationed items. As a result of the inevitable shortages caused by the war, people in Northern Ireland made trips to Dublin to purchase essentials and luxuries. In spite of their antipathy to the border, many people took the opportunity to benefit financially from its existence.

THE SMUGGLERS' EXPRESS.

'The Smugglers' Express', Maskee, *Dublin Opinion*, Dublin, March 1942

As the war years came to a close, a Catholic northerner, writing under the pseudonym 'Ultach', set out the reality of life in Northern Ireland under a unionist government. His exposé struck a deeply pessimistic note: 'I live [here]. Not only do I experience the effects of persecution which is the dominant feature of life [here] but I know the people who vote for, support, and benefit . . . from the continuance of the regime.'

'Orange Terror', Ultach, *Capuchin Annual*, Dublin, 1943

THE POSTWAR YEARS

In the immediate aftermath of the Second World War, relations between Northern Ireland and the Irish Free State continued to be less than cordial. The root of the problem was still the partition of the island, and the existence of two separate and independent governments. The fears and aspirations of both states were embodied in the persons of their respective leaders, Sir Basil Brooke, who had succeeded John Andrews as prime minister in 1943, and Eamon de Valera. While the two heads of state generally ignored each other personally, the ingredients of a political and ideological dogfight were ever present.

'Petty Politics – Political Dog Show', Bell, *PTQ*, Belfast, 1946

Within Northern Ireland, relations between the Protestant and unionist population, and the Catholic and (mainly) nationalist community, were also less than cordial. The passage of the 1947 Education Act through the parliament at Stormont revealed the antipathy that existed between the two communities. In essence, the Act provided secondary school education for all from the age of eleven to fifteen, and provided a state grant of 65 per cent for school buildings and their maintenance. It also ended compulsory Bible instruction in state schools. The immediate and obvious benefits to postwar education in Northern Ireland were ignored in the religious furore that greeted the passing of the Act. The Catholic Church saw it as an attempt to weaken its control over its flock; and the Protestant churches saw it as an endowment of Catholic education. Most worrying for the churches, however, was that the sectarian nature of education provision in Northern Ireland would, in theory, be ended by the Act. A committee appointed at a public meeting in Belfast to secure amendments to the Act published its concerns in *The Defence of Ulster*: 'Roman Catholics and Secularism are a constant menace . . . This menace has been much increased by the

'The Exams are Over', PTQ, Belfast, 1947

passing of the new Education Act (1947) . . .' What had been designed as a passport to a better future for the children of Northern Ireland also served to display to the world the strange and sectarian nature of the state and its people. Then, as now, students themselves were more concerned with the pressures of study and exams than with their religious content.

Affairs in Northern Ireland were being watched with concern in Westminster. A debate in the House of Commons to extend the duration of the Special Powers Act in respect of Northern Ireland gave opposition MPs the opportunity to discuss the manner in which the country was being governed. In a preamble to his speech on the topic, Geoffrey Bing, MP for Hornchurch, raised a number of concerns:

> Before this House can agree to grant additional powers to the Parliament of Northern Ireland . . . [we] need to be satisfied on three points. [Are] the dictatorial powers at present exercised by the Home Secretary of Northern Ireland . . . justified, or [are] they . . . merely a weapon against political opponents? [Are] the express provisions of Sections 5 and 8 of the Government of Northern Ireland Act against religious discrimination or [are they] fostering religious discrimination for party purposes? In Northern Ireland [are] both Parliamentary and local elections . . . democratically and fairly conducted?

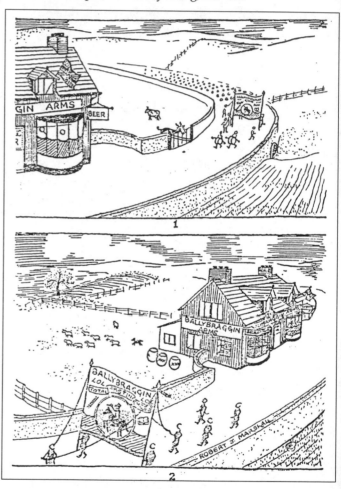

'Ballybraggin LOL', Marshall, PTQ, Belfast, 1947

Hornchurch cited this remark made by the prime minister of Northern Ireland to justify his concerns: 'I recommend people not to employ Roman Catholics who are 99 per cent disloyal . . .' Such a comment, and others delivered at gatherings of Orangemen at Twelfth of July celebrations, he contended, were at variance with the principles of democracy.

Easy to Grasp

'Easy to Grasp', CEK, *Dublin Opinion*, Dublin, April 1948

Others, closer to home, also believed that a redrafting of the Better Government of Ireland Act was necessary. The newly elected taoiseach of the Free State, John A. Costello, began to make friendly overtures to his northern counterpart, Sir Basil Brooke, in an attempt to achieve better relations between the two states, and to improve the condition of northern nationalists.

Such overtures met with little encouragement in Northern Ireland, and this prompted some individuals and groups to suggest more radical measures. The little known, and short-lived, Ulster Union Club put forward the traditionally republican alternative to the political status quo – a single parliament for the whole of Ireland. In its 1949 pamphlet, *Unionism or Unity?: A Suggested New Deal for Six-County Industry*, it proposed a 'transfer of the powers to legislate for the six counties at present reserved to the Parliament at Westminster to an All Ireland Parliament: the six counties to be constituted a federal portion of the Irish Nation . . .' The prime minister, created Lord Brookeborough in 1947, and the unionists of Northern Ireland remained, however, staunchly opposed to any change to the border.

"How about a wee Iron Curtain, Sir Basil?"

'How about . . .?', Friers, *Dublin Opinion*, Dublin, May 1948

" The penalty is a little hard at this particular post ! "

'The penalty is a little hard . . .', Friers, *Dublin Opinion*, Dublin, August 1947

To reaffirm its constitutional position, the government of Northern Ireland, through Conservative and Unionist Central Office, produced a pamphlet entitled *Ulster Is British: A Re-affirmation of Ulster's Political Outlook*, a reasoned apologia for the existence of the state of Northern Ireland. Published in 1949 and solely for private circulation, the pamphlet rehearsed the events which brought the state into being, and set out the determination of the unionist people to remain a part of the United Kingdom:

> The foregoing memorandum has aimed to make clear that the determined wish of the majority in Northern Ireland is to retain their British connection. Yet, despite the 1920 Act, the 1921 London Treaty and the 1925 Three Party Agreement, the whole constitutional position of Ulster is being continually questioned in the South . . . The advocacy of force was hinted at by Mr DeValera . . . to which Sir Basil Brooke replied: 'I feel justified in throwing it back in his teeth and in telling him he can use what force he wants, but he will never get Ulster . . .'

**Sir Romeo Brooke (to Juliet Ni Houlihan): 'For $^6/_{32}$ of
you darling, I would gladly lay down my life!'**

'Sir Romeo Brooke . . .', CEK, *Dublin Opinion*, Dublin, November 1948

The frustration of northern Catholics and nationalists at their virtual disenfranchisement in a predominantly Protestant and unionist state caused bitterness and disaffection. In 1949 Eddie McAteer, MP for Mid-Derry, published a paper entitled 'Irish Action: New Thoughts on an Old Subject', which was based on his understanding of the political philosophy of Mahatma Gandhi, whose peaceful tactics had been instrumental in achieving the independence of India from colonial Britain. The programme of 'non-cooperation and non-violence' which McAteer endorsed was designed to frustrate and obstruct the effective government of Northern Ireland, while doing as much as possible to bankrupt it. The paper stated:

> The old boycott idea springs to mind . . . and it must be practised to the maximum . . . All pro-British functions must be shunned like the plague . . . All [government] forms must be lost and if needs be you can cause the Department concerned to issue a duplicate. Not much, of course, but it still tends to harass them . . . A note of caution. If completion of these forms brings financial benefit . . . then complete them by all means . . .

Small wonder then that Lord Brookeborough was able to resist the blandishments of the anti-Partition League and the overtures of his southern counterpart.

'We picked a Rugby Team that way and it worked very well.'

'We picked a rugby team . . .', CEK, *Dublin Opinion*, Dublin, April 1949   83

The Baby Sitter

'The Baby Sitter', CEK, *Dublin Opinion*, Dublin, June 1949

In June 1949, Prime Minister Clement Attlee tried to strengthen the unionist position by guaranteeing the constitutional position of Northern Ireland. This was provided for in the Ireland Act which affirmed that 'in no event will Northern Ireland or any part thereof cease to be part of His Majesty's dominions and of the United Kingdom without the consent of the parliament of Northern Ireland'.

The guarantee was anathema to northern nationalists and southern anti-partitionists, who characterised it as 'the dismemberment of one of the most ancient nations in Europe'. They condemned it as the 'the act of a stranger',

'Well spoken, gentlemen!'

'Well spoken, gentlemen', CEK, *Dublin Opinion*, Dublin, June 1949   85

and designated Northern Ireland 'a bloody pawn in a party game'. The history and the consequences of partition were aired at an all-party, anti-partition meeting in Dublin in May 1949. Speaker after speaker explained how partition had damaged Ireland north and south:

> The six counties have lost immeasurably by Partition. In the inter-war years . . . the economic situation in the partitioned area was so deplorable that subsidies from Britain were required to keep the Government afloat. In the war years, the Six Counties had to send enormous sums to Britain . . . as an Imperial contribution, thus dispersing [its] resources . . . Situated as it is, without free access to its natural markets in Ireland, the partitioned area cannot expect prosperity . . . Because the minority is permanently persecuted in an effort to compel then to accept a permanently inferior position and acquiesce in their separation from their own countrymen, there are not the conditions necessary for internal peace . . .

" THE TWELFTH," 1690 (B.C.)

'The Twelfth', Colm, *PTQ*, Belfast, 1950

Unionist reaction to such arguments was to ignore them where possible, reaffirm the validity of their own history and traditions, and elevate their own cultural heritage within the northern state.

Blow a bit easier, Carmichael, I can't hear what I'm drummin !

'Blow a bit easier . . . ', Achie, *PTQ*, Belfast, 1949

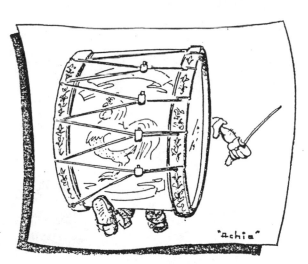

**Portrait of Willie John Mackswickle on
"The Twelfth."**

'Portrait of Willie John . . . ', Achie, *PTQ*, Belfast, 1950

The underlying reality of partition, however, was deeply embedded in the psyche of the people of Ireland. As the presence of the map on the back wall shows, partition infused and informed all areas of life, north and south.

THE DEPARTMENT OF AGRICULTURE, NEW STYLE
(*As imagined by Our Grangegorman Correspondent*)

'The Department of Agriculture, New Style',
CEK, *Dublin Opinion*, Dublin, April 1950

Lady Brooke: 'Who is the lady with the lamp?'
Sir Basil: 'Florence Nightingale, I imagine, my dear.'

'Who is the lady with the lamp?', CEK, *Dublin Opinion*, Dublin, May 1950

On both sides, politicians and people believed that they were right, and that their political opponents were gratuitously perverse, if not evil, in maintaining their counter position. It was easy with such a mindset to vilify your neighbour.

At rare times, however, practical politics and cooperation could be undertaken by the two governments. In June 1950, the governments of Northern Ireland and the Republic of Ireland separately and jointly passed the Erne Drainage and Development Acts, which allowed both parts of Ireland to cooperate in a joint scheme of drainage and electricity generation. These acts produced hitherto unimagined benefits for the rural communities in both political jurisdictions in Ireland and inaugurated a quiet revolution in the living standards of those who worked the land.

Idyll

'During the debate on the Erne Drainage and Development Bill, which was given a second reading by the Northern Ireland Senate, Mr P. J. O'Hare said that commonsense and goodwill had enabled both the Northern and Southern Governments to rise above the absurdity of the Border.' – *Irish Times*

'Idyll', CEK, *Dublin Opinion*, Dublin, July 1950

THE DERRY AIR
'You know, Jan, from up here it looks very like one country to me!'

'The Derry Air', CEK, *Dublin Opinion*, Dublin, February 1951

Such joint ventures between the governments of Northern Ireland and the Irish Republic suggested to foreign political observers that the vexed question of partition would eventually be resolved by the appreciation of the mutual benefits of cooperation.

This was not to be the case. As a physical emblem of partition, the border remained one of the most potent symbols of disunity in the island of Ireland. It was also one of the enduring realities of life for both populations. The economic benefits of a territorial barrier in a small country could (and did) swing to the advantage of either state at different times.

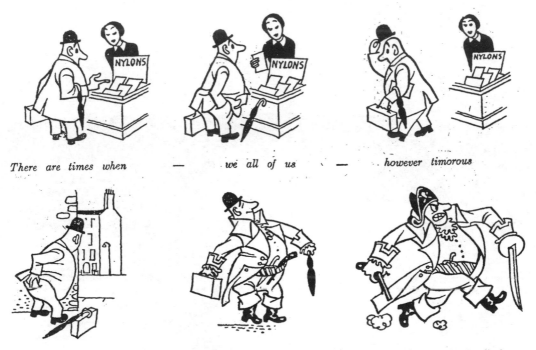

There are times when — we all of us — however timorous

like to imagine — we are bold bad villains at heart — and every bit as daredevil as our boyhood's heroes.

But, face us with reality . . . !

'Customs', Friers, *Dublin Opinion*, Dublin, August 1951

INGENIOUS DEVICE FOR ENDING PARTITION

'Ingenious Device for Ending Partition', Friers, *Dublin Opinion*, Dublin, May 1951　　93

'Guns in Ulster', Clark, *Guns in Ulster*, Belfast, 1967

In the 1950s, a new generation of young and militant republicans, frustrated by, and contemptuous of, the lack of success of the Anti-Partition League, resorted to the bomb and the bullet in an attempt to end the partition of Ireland. Border raids, attacks on police barracks and military installations occurred as small bands of IRA men waged sporadic terror over the next ten years in an attempt to achieve a United Ireland. Unionist reaction was to reinforce the Special Constabulary and to step up patrols, checkpoints, and night raids on suspected terrorists.

When de Valera became president of the Irish Republic in 1959, he was determined to prevent the IRA from using the South as a base to make incursions into Northern Ireland. He re-introduced internment and starved the movement of weapons, ammunition and money. Faced with two determined governments, skilled in the tactics of self-preservation, the IRA's border campaign was called off in February 1962.

'RUC', MacNeil, *PTQ*, Belfast, 1953

'Captain O'Neill', McBride,
Belfast Telegraph, Belfast, 24 May 1957

CAPTAIN O'NEILL
—acquits himself with ease.

Mr. HUNTER
—For schoolchildren the Ulster
past is generally a blank.

'Mr Hunter', McBride, *Belfast Telegraph*,
Belfast, 31 May 1957

'Captain Henderson', McBride,
Belfast Telegraph, 1 March 1957

CAPTAIN HENDERSON
—Concerned about security.

Throughout the fifties, parliamentary life in Northern Ireland continued. Health, education, housing, transport, agriculture and fisheries all needed to be managed, as did security. Captain Terence O'Neill, minister of finance, Captain O.W.S. Henderson, unionist member for Victoria ward, and Captain Alexander Hunter, unionist member for Carrick, were some of the unionist parliamentarians from this period.

'Mr Healy', McBride, *Belfast Telegraph*,
Belfast, 22 February 1957

MR. HEALY—*he walked out.*

The futility of opposition in the northern parliament was epitomised in the careers of men such as Cahir Healy, Nationalist member for Fermanagh, who was a thorn in the side of the unionist government without achieving any of his nationalist aims; and Harry Midgley, who began political life as secretary of the Northern Ireland Labour Party before joining the Unionist Party in 1947, and becoming minister of education in 1950. Outside the Unionist Party there was no political advancement.

'Mr Midgley's reply . . .', McBride,
Belfast Telegraph, Belfast, 16 April 1956

" *Mr. Midgley's reply was brief,
but no less effective.*"

" Still nursing the unconquerable hope . . ."
—*Matthew Arnold*

'Still nursing the unconquerable hope . . .', CEK, *Dublin Opinion,,* Dublin, November 1959

Relations between Northern Ireland and the Irish Republic remained difficult, particularly over the issue of partition. Seán Lemass, who became taoiseach in June 1959, was a younger and more dynamic leader than de Valera and much more open to discussion and negotiation. In a speech at a meeting of the Oxford Union Society on 15 October 1959, the possibility of re-unification was broached along innovative lines:

It has been proposed that the question of Irish reunification . . . be considered on the basis of an arrangement under which the Parliament and Government of Northern Ireland would continue to function with their present powers, while an all-Ireland Parliament would exercise the powers in relation to that area now exercised at Westminster.

Lord Brookeborough, still prime minister of Northern Ireland, was, however, unreceptive and remained deeply entrenched in a nostalgic unionism.

'Sir Basil, Sir Sean', JOD, *Dublin Opinion*, Dublin, December 1959

Mr. Gerry Mander
(*A Recent Photograph*)

'Mr Gerry Mander', CEK, *Dublin Opinion*, Dublin, March 1959

Those who lived in other parts of the United Kingdom, and who wished to understand what was happening in Northern Ireland, were poorly served by central government or the media during the 1950s and 1960s. *The Spectator*, for example, in 1961, argued that sectarianism was not neccessarily a bad thing: 'Englishmen who shudder at the thought of the deep religious division rarely understand the compensating homogenousness until they have lived in Ulster . . .' Meanwhile, in Northern Ireland, resentment among the Catholic community was growing. The allocation of local government housing, the imbalance in government employment, and the manipulation of electoral boundaries to allow a unionist minority to control the predominantly Catholic and nationalist city of Derry created tensions that would inevitably lead to community violence.

In such a climate even the question of whether Britain and Northern Ireland should join the Common Market was liable to have a sectarian edge.

NOT A CENTIMETRE!
'We must . . . all ask ourselves what is the function of the Orange Institution in a Common Market.' DR NIXON

'Not a Centimetre!',
ERH, *Review: An Ulster Political Commentary*, Belfast, October 1962

Of much more fundamental importance was the seeming drift towards a new, friendly and cooperative future with the people and parliament of the Irish Republic. Much of the reason for this lay in the fact that Lord Brookeborough had been replaced in 1963 by Captain Terence O'Neill, a more open and conciliatory leader. That immense progress in relations had been achieved was clear when, in 1965, O'Neill and Taoiseach Seán Lemass had lunch at Stormont. Later that year, O'Neill and Lemass met in Dublin to discuss topics of mutual interest and concern. The tentative improvement in North–South relations infuriated hardline unionists such as the Reverend Ian Paisley, who was concurrently combating the 'Romeward' trend in the Presbyterian Church in Northern Ireland. He spoke in strident terms to a constituency always suspicious of their Catholic and nationalist neighbour. In June 1966, another instance of the underlying sectarian hatreds that existed in Ulster manifested itself when a young Catholic barman was shot and murdered in Malvern Street, in the Shankill Road area of Belfast, by members of the loyalist paramilitary group, the Ulster Volunteer Force. Within a short space of time, community conflict had reached an unprecedented level, and whole areas of Belfast and Derry had been barricaded off to try to stem the escalating violence.

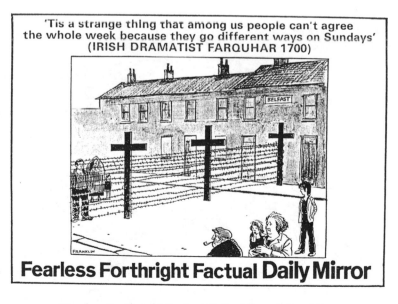

'Fearless Forthright Factual Daily Mirror', Franklin,
Socialist Commentary, London, October 1969

THE TROUBLES
1969–2000

The growing violence and civil unrest in Northern Ireland
in the 1960s was initially overshadowed by more global
concerns. Britain's attempt to join the Common Market and
De Gaulle's determination that they should not; America's
involvement in the conflict in Vietnam; Rhodesia's racist
policies; unrest in the Middle East: these were the topics that
exercised the minds of world leaders in the late 1960s.

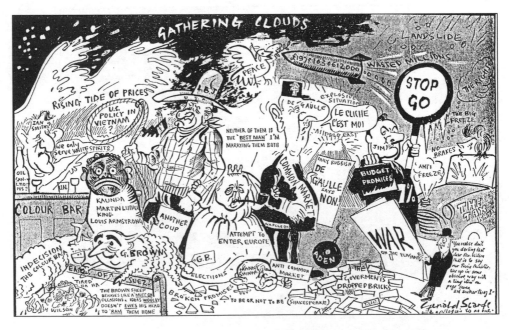

'Gathering Clouds', Scarfe, *New Statesman*, London, 28 April 1967

However, the prime minister of Northern Ireland, Captain Terence O'Neill, was faced with a deteriorating situation, unprecedented in the history of the state. Civil rights marches – in Derry in October 1968, and from Belfast to Derry in January 1969 – exposed to a world audience the sectarian tensions and violence of a divided state. The attack on a People's Democracy march at Burntollet Bridge was beamed into homes across the world, and O'Neill's government stood indicted. Tentative moves towards reform brought open opposition within his own party and, as violence spread, unionist back-benchers called for his resignation. In April 1969, in the wake of a series of terrorist attacks on public buildings, and realising that he had lost the support of his own party, O'Neill resigned.

'Captain Terence O'Neill', Willson, *Spectator*, London, 24 January 1969

O'Neill's successor, Major James Chichester-Clarke, was immediately faced with the problem of bolstering support for government policy in the face of mounting opposition.

"And for the next trick I need help from the audience."

'And for the next trick . . .', Friers, *Riotous Living*, Belfast, 1971

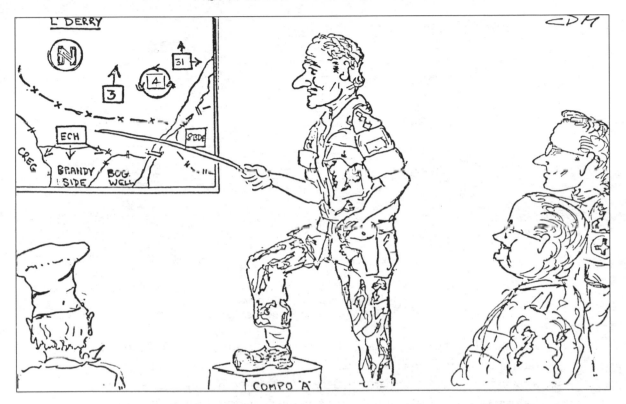

'AS I SEE IT, DUFFY AND THE COOKS WILL TAKE BRANDYSIDE, POSTY AND BOSCO THE CREGGAN, CHIEFY AND THE CLERKS . . .'

'QM(T) on His Daily Planning Conference', CDM, *By'eeeee the right . . . Laugh*, Belfast, 1973

Sectarian attacks throughout July and August 1969 prompted appeals from Stormont to Westminster to send troops to relieve a beleaguered RUC. On 14 August 1969, a company of the Prince of Wales Own Regiment began a tour of duty in Derry. Initially, their understanding of the geography of the city, never mind the complexities of the political situation, was slightly hazy.

The barricades must come down',
Homer, *New Statesman*, London, 19 September 1969

As makeshift barricades went up in various, mainly nationalist areas of Belfast and Derry, Chichester-Clarke declared the need for a specially constructed 'peace line' in parts of Belfast to keep both communities apart. Reform of the Special Constabulary saw the disbandment of the B Specials in April 1970, amidst widespread unionist protest, and the inauguration of the Ulster Defence Regiment. In January of the same year, the worsening situation had led to a split in the republican movement and to the formation of the Provisional IRA, who were dissatisfied with Official IRA tactics for removing the British presence from Northern Ireland. Nationalist opinion, however, was largely focused in the Social Democratic and Labour Party, founded by Gerry Fitt, John Hume, Austin Curry, Ivan Cooper and Paddy Devlin in August 1970. Chichester-Clarke's inability to deal effectively with developing events turned him into an increasingly marginalised and ineffective figure. He resigned his position in March 1971, having failed to secure extra British troops to effect a military occupation of urban no-go areas. The cartoon above also shows the figure of Ian Paisley, who was particularly critical of Chichester-Clarke. Coming to prominence in the sixties, Paisley was to become a vociferous and entrenched defender of the cause of loyalists in Northern Ireland.

Untitled, *Hibernia*, Dublin, 8 October 1971

Chichester-Clarke was succeeded by possibly the most able, but least trust-ed, unionist politician of his day, Brian Faulkner. Faulkner set about restor-ing order as quickly as possible, amidst escalating community violence, the murder of policemen by paramilitary terrorists, and the wholesale destruc-tion of public and commercial property. His first resort was to the tried and trusted method of internment without trial, which was introduced in August 1971. This measure, in turn, sparked off further protests and vio-lence, and occasioned a summit meeting at Chequers between Taoiseach Jack Lynch, British Prime Minister Edward Heath and Northern Irish Prime Minister Brian Faulkner. Their deliberations proved fruitless.

'Extremism', Friers, *Belfast Telegraph*, Belfast, 27 March 1971

Faulkner was beset by some of the worst violence of the troubles. In December 1971, a bomb at McGurk's bar in North Queen Street in Belfast killed fifteen people and injured many more. In January of the following year, thirteen unarmed civilians were killed in Derry when the Parachute Regiment opened fire on a civil rights march. In March 1972 a bomb in the crowded Abercorn restaurant in the centre of Belfast killed two and injured 130 people. As a result of the continuing violence, Heath summoned Faulkner to London to discuss the situation. It was clear that Stormont could no longer control the state of Northern Ireland and, on 30 March 1972, direct rule from Westminster was introduced. Faulkner, aware from the outset that the deteriorating situation needed firm leadership, was defeated by the enormity and complexity of the divisions in Northern Irish society.

Under direct rule, the first secretary of state for Northern Ireland was William Whitelaw. His arrival in Northern Ireland was marked by a two-day strike, organised by William Craig's Ulster Vanguard movement. Edward Heath, in a televised address to the people of Northern Ireland, explained the opportunity presented by direct rule: 'Now is your chance. A chance for fairness, a chance for prosperity, a chance for peace, a chance at last to bring the bombings and the killings to an end . . .' That chance was spurned for another three decades.

'The Last Chance Saloon', Friers, *Belfast Telegraph*, Belfast, 1 April 1972

'Come on fellas, pull together and we'll be getting somewhere.'

'Come on fellas . . .', Friers, *Irish Times*, Dublin, 15 October 1973

Seeking a political solution to the troubles in Northern Ireland, the government published a White Paper in March 1973 entitled 'Northern Ireland Constitutional Proposals'. The document called for a Northern Ireland assembly elected by proportional representation, whose executive must reflect the different communities within Northern Ireland society. There was also a strong North–South element in the proposals. Elections to the assembly took place in June 1973 and produced a clear majority in favour of power sharing. The first meeting of the assembly took place in July 1973, but Faulkner insisted from the outset that he was not prepared to participate in a power-sharing executive unless unionists were guaranteed a majority of seats and, therefore, power. Above, William Whitelaw tries to encourage dejected politicians such as Brian Faulkner, far left, and Paddy Devlin, far right, into participating in a power-sharing agreement.

'Power Sharing', *Hibernia*, Dublin, 14 December 1973

Discussions on the implementation of power sharing led to the formation of an executive in November 1973. In December 1973 a tripartite conference was held at Sunningdale in Berkshire to agree relationships between Britain, the Republic of Ireland and Northern Ireland. In the face of continuing and substantial opposition, unionist and nationalist leaders tried to play up the gains that would result from such an innovative political initiative. Above, from right to left, are Brian Faulkner, William Whitelaw, Gerry Fitt, Ian Paisley and John Hume, all key players in the debate about power sharing.

As soon as the details of the Sunningdale Agreement were made known, loyalist paramilitaries formed the Ulster Army Council to oppose power sharing and the Council of Ireland. Their actions culminated in the Ulster Workers' Council strike of May 1974, which saw a virtual shut-down of industry and electrical supplies throughout Northern Ireland. Faced with such widespread chaos, Merlyn Rees, who had replaced Whitelaw as secretary of state, announced a state of emergency, but the strikers had already won the day. On 28 May 1974 Brian Faulkner resigned as chief executive of the Northern Ireland assembly, and the power-sharing executive ceased to exist.

'The Sunningdale Mess', Oisín, *Andersonstown News*, Belfast, 18 May 1975

With the fall of the executive, community violence escalated and, in an effort to bring perpetrators to justice, resort was made to Diplock courts, judge-only trials, where the uncorroborated evidence of police witnesses was accepted. This deviation from the norm of British judicial procedure was persisted in because of the widespread intimidation of witnesses and jurors by paramilitary and terrorist groups.

GREAT FUN! GREAT FUN! IS THAT IT FOR TO-DAY - YER HONOR?

'Special Court', Oisín, *Andersonstown News*, Belfast, 1975

A political solution was still being sought. The Westminster government, now led by Harold Wilson, pushed through legislation replacing the former assembly and executive with an elected Constitutional Convention. Elections to the Convention went ahead on 1 May 1975, but with unionists gaining 47 of the 78 seats, and many still hostile to even the concept of power sharing, the future of the Convention looked bleak.

'Don't rock it . . .', Oisín, *Andersonstown News*, Belfast, 1975

'Born in a Fenian Ghetto?' Cormac, *An Phoblacht/Republican News*,
Belfast, 7 June 1980

Debate within the Convention was acrimonious and sterile, and could
arrive at a no more innovative recommendation than a return to single-
party domination of the parliament of Northern Ireland. This was obvious-
ly unacceptable to those parties, notably the SDLP, who supported power
sharing. Westminster now realised that effective direct rule for the foresee-
able future was the only way forward. In March 1976 the secretary of state
revoked the special category status which allowed those committing terrorist offences the status of political prisoners. Under the new regime, prisoners convicted of terrorist offences were made to wear prison clothing.
Republican prisoners were deeply hostile and refused to cooperate with
prison authorities.

Angered at this attempt to 'criminalise' and denigrate their political motivation, republican prisoners made numerous escape bids, not only to gain personal freedom but also as a propaganda coup for their organisation. In May 1976 nine Irish Republican Socialist Party prisoners escaped from the Maze prison on the outskirts of Lisburn, County Antrim.

"Call that a Maze?"

'Call that a Maze?', Friers, *Belfast Telegraph*, Belfast, 29 September 1973

The political situation had reached stalemate, and violence continued unabated. In this atmosphere, one of Northern Ireland's best-known politicians, Brian Faulkner, announced his retirement from public life. His leaving was duly noted by a divided and ungenerous community.

..... AND ALL THE QUEEN'S MEN COULDN'T PUT HUMPTY DUMPTY TOGETHER AGAIN!

'And All the Queen's Men . . .', Oisín, *Andersonstown News*, Belfast, 1 June 1974

He was followed from the Northern Ireland stage by Merlyn Rees who was replaced as secretary of state in September 1976 by Roy Mason. Mason now took on the thankless task of trying to mediate between the warring factions in Northern Ireland.

'Provos . . . UUC . . . SDLP . . . UDA', Friers, *Irish Times*, Dublin, 18 September 1976

'Let there be no light', Friers, *Irish Times*, Dublin, 14 May 1977

Mason's chief of police, Kenneth Newman, had seen service in Palestine, and was of the opinion that strong policing and a reduction in army presence on the streets were essential to the regularisation of community life. The resolve of both men was to be tested early in 1977, when a campaign to restore majority rule at Stormont was launched by the Reverend Ian Paisley. Backed by the United Unionist Action Council, a coalition of loyalist groupings, Paisley gave Mason an ultimatum: either he implement the Convention Report and have an all-out onslaught against republican terrorists, or the UUAC would bring Northern Ireland to its knees by calling out the power workers as in 1974. Mason and Newman stood firm against this threat, and when the power workers at Ballylumford power station refused to give their support, the 'constitutional stoppage' foundered. Paisley was reduced to having a token stoppage of Ballymena town centre, which was soon cleared by the army and police.

Mason was able to report that 1977 had been a year of unprecedented success, with the facing down of a second loyalist strike, and a dramatic reduction in violence and loss of life. Speaking in December of that year to the *Daily Express* he boasted that 'the tide had turned against the terrorists, and the message for 1978 [is] one of hope'. He could not have been more wrong. On the evening of 17 February 1978, the IRA planted two firebombs at the La Mon House Hotel between Belfast and Comber in County Down. When they detonated, a huge fireball engulfed the function rooms. Twelve people died, and twenty-three others were horribly burned.

'The Road to La Mon', Friers, *Belfast Telegraph*, Belfast, 25 February 1978

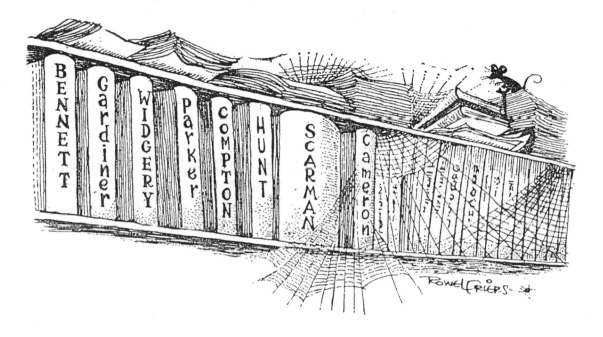

'Bennett . . .', Friers, *Irish Times*, Dublin, 24 March 1979

This horrific attack was seen as a direct terrorist response to Mason's claims of increasing security force success against the IRA. Interrogation techniques at Castlereagh and Gough barracks had been very successful in garnering information of IRA structures, tactics and plans, and had been directly responsible for the reduction in IRA activity. But these techniques were deemed inhumane by Amnesty International. Mason was forced to order an investigation and Judge Harry Bennett was asked to conduct the inquiry. His report, published in March 1979, was highly critical, and recommended a number of reforms. Mason's failure to implement these recommendations angered the leader of the SDLP, Gerry Fitt, who withdrew his support from the Labour government at Westminster.

'Pantomine Time Again', Oisín, *Andersonstown News*, Belfast, 29 December 1979

Ironically, a fortnight later, a vote of no confidence in the Labour government was passed by a majority of one. Prime Minister James Callaghan, forced to go to the polls in May 1979, was heavily defeated. A Conservative government took power, led by Margaret Thatcher. Her choice for secretary of state for Northern Ireland was a relative unknown – Humphrey Atkins. Both were to have a baptism of fire in their new posts. On 27 August 1979 the IRA planted a bomb on the dual carriageway between Newry and Warrenpoint in County Down, killing eighteen members of the Parachute Regiment. On the same day they planted a bomb on a boat at Mullaghmore in County Sligo in the Republic of Ireland, killing Earl Mountbatten and three others. Thatcher visited security forces in Northern Ireland to be briefed on the situation. She resisted demands for a tougher military response, and encouraged Atkins to pursue a political accommodation between the polarised politicians in Northern Ireland. In October 1979 Atkins called a round table conference of all political parties to discuss and agree a new and acceptable form of devolved government in Northern Ireland. The White Paper, which set out the parameters of discussion, angered the SDLP because it had no 'Irish dimension'. Gerry Fitt, frustrated at his party's stance on the White Paper, resigned as party leader, and was replaced by John Hume.

The Ulster Unionist Party, led by James Molyneaux, refused to join the discussions at all. In spite of this, round table talks continued, but it was obvious that they were doomed not to succeed. By November 1980, they had failed.

'Blankety Blank', Friers, *Belfast Telegraph*, Belfast, 6 December 1980

'It's no fun . . .', Cormac, *An Phoblacht/Republican News*, Belfast, 10 December 1981

Thatcher now turned her attention to the Dublin government and in December, she flew to the southern capital to hold talks with the Fianna Fáil leader and taoiseach, Charles Haughey. The meeting was a success, and a joint communiqué spoke of further meetings to discuss 'the totality of relationships within these islands'. Such a strategy dismayed unionists. The Reverend Ian Paisley was appalled, and immediately set out to wreck the initiative. In February 1981, journalists were taken to see five hundred uniformed men on a hillside near Ballymena, County Antrim. These men constituted Paisley's Third Force, dedicated to defend loyalist and unionist hegemony in Northern Ireland.

'Point of order Mr Speaker . . .', Friers, *Irish Times*, Dublin, 4 April 1981

The breakdown of talks between Thatcher and Haughey, however, was occasioned not by Paisley's Third Force, but by happenings within the Maze prison. In March 1981 republican prisoners had gone on hunger strike in an attempt to have their 'special category' status returned. Their leader was Bobby Sands, who first refused food on 1 March. In April, Sands stood in the by-election in Fermanagh–South Tyrone, brought about by the death of the sitting MP, Frank Maguire. Amidst intense international attention, Sands was elected. At that point he had been on hunger strike for forty days.

Twenty-six days later, Bobby Sands died in prison, refusing all appeals to end his hunger strike. Atkins and the British government remained inflexible in their attitude to 'special category' status and the hunger strikes by republican prisoners continued. In all, ten prisoners died on hunger strike, the last, Michael Devlin, on 20 August 1981. Widespread community violence accompanied each death. In September, during a cabinet reshuffle, Atkins was replaced as secretary of state by James Prior.

'So farewell then . . .', Cormac,
An Phoblacht/Republican News, Belfast, 19 September 1981

'Ballot Box', Friers, *Irish Times*, Dublin, 27 February 1982

Prior quickly made contact with representatives of the republican prisoners and hinted at concessions. On 30 October 1981 the hunger strikes were called off. Prior announced that in future prisoners could wear their own clothes, that half of their lost remission would be restored to them, and that prison visits and internal communication would be enhanced. Later that year, in a rhetorical flourish at the annual conference or *ard fheis* of Provisional Sinn Féin in Dublin's Mansion House, Danny Morrison moved the party towards participation in the democratic process in Northern Ireland when he referred to the election of Sands earlier in the year. He asked Sinn Féin delegates, 'Will anyone here object if with a ballot box in this hand and an Armalite in this hand we take power in Ireland?' This strategy, endorsed by the *ard fheis*, began the slow, tortuous process which would eventually see Sinn Féin enter constitutional politics some twenty years later.

In February 1981 the secretary of state presented a new initiative for Northern Ireland known as 'rolling devolution'. This involved the setting up of an advisory assembly, with executive powers being devolved only when cross-community consensus had been reached. In spite of the fact that none of the main Northern Ireland parties or the Conservative government at Westminster was in favour of the proposals, elections took place in October 1982. Sinn Féin, pursuing their twin-track approach of Armalite and ballot box, won 10 per cent of first-preference votes, mainly at the expense of the SDLP. Both nationalist parties boycotted the proceedings of the assembly, and the ill-starred initiative collapsed.

'Advisory Assembly – All Welcome', Friers, *Irish Times*, Dublin, 27 September 1980

'The Irish', JAK, *Evening Standard*, London, 29 October 1982

The killings and bombings continued in Northern Ireland, and the political vacuum persisted. The British public, intimately and emotionally involved in the conflict with Argentina over the Falkland Islands, were at a loss to understand, never mind resolve, the sectarian and political conflict in neighbouring Northern Ireland. The horrific loss of life in the IRA bombing of the Droppin' Well public house in Ballykelly, County Derry, only reinforced a sense of bewilderment and outrage in Britain.

In the 1983 general election Gerry Adams defeated Gerry Fitt in West Belfast and went on to become president of Sinn Féin. With Sinn Féin and the SDLP both holding one seat each in the Westminster parliament, the possibility now presented itself that Sinn Féin might replace the SDLP as the representative voice of the nationalist community. Fitt was appointed a peer in the House of Lords, much to the disgust of republicans.

'Fitt is a Brit', Littleman, *Magill*, Dublin, July 1983

In the face of growing support for Sinn Féin, the New Ireland Forum, brainchild of John Hume and the Fine Gael Taoiseach Garret FitzGerald, met throughout 1983 and early 1984. Made up mostly of nationalists – the UUP had refused to join – it brought together those parties who were committed to the idea of a 'new Ireland' and to achieving that aim within the framework of constitutional politics. It presented its findings in May 1984. Three options were identified and outlined – a unitary state, a federal arrangement, or joint sovereignty. Unionists rejected the report out of hand, and Westminster was undecided. In October 1984 an event occurred which focused attention on the necessity of resolving the Northern Ireland problem: an IRA bomb ripped through the Grand Hotel, Brighton, during the Conservative Party conference. Five people were killed and many injured, including Norman Tebbit, Conservative Party chairman and close friend and confidant of the prime minister.

"YOU WERE LUCKY THIS TIME . . . YOU WON'T BE LUCKY NEXT TIME."
– THE IRA

'You were lucky this time . . .', Cookson, *Sun*, London, 13 October 1984

AFTER THE AGREEMENT

'After the Agreement', Hamilton, *Fortnight*, Belfast, 2–15 December 1985

At an inter-governmental meeting, Thatcher and FitzGerald discussed in detail possible paths to a solution of the political impasse in Northern Ireland. The press conference which followed seemed to show that they were unable to reach agreement on a way forward, but further meetings resulted in a dramatic and unprecedented joint communiqué at Hillsborough Castle, County Down, on 15 November 1985. The Anglo-Irish Agreement sought to legitimise nationalist aspirations for a united Ireland while, at the same time, reaffirming the union of Northern Ireland and Britain for as long as it remained the will of the people of Northern Ireland. The Agreement also acknowledged the legitimacy of a North–South dimension to any solution.

The SDLP and the middle-of-the-road Alliance Party supported the Agreement, Sinn Féin and all colours of unionism rejected it. At a mass rally in central Belfast at least 50,000 anti-Agreement unionists demonstrated their opposition. In December 1985, all unionist MPs resigned from Westminster in protest. A campaign of civil disobedience soon deteriorated into violence aimed principally at the Royal Ulster Constabulary, and in the face of its patent failure to function, the assembly at Stormont was wound up in June 1986, four years after it had begun. In the cartoon below, a unionist family gathering led by James Molyneaux, leader of the Official Unionists, is disrupted by the arrival of Seamus Mallon of the SDLP.

'Ripping Yarns . . .', Blotski, *Fortnight*, Belfast, September 1986

Although anti-Agreement demonstrations by loyalists took place throughout Northern Ireland, the British government refused to capitulate. Support for the Agreement grew steadily in the Irish Republic, where Charles Haughey, now taoiseach, fully supported its provisions. The IRA reacted to the Agreement with an even more vicious campaign of murder and terror, particularly against anyone giving assistance to the army and the RUC. Security force reaction was in kind. In May 1987 eight IRA men were killed in an abortive attack on Loughgall police station: their plan of attack had been betrayed to the RUC. This loss of personnel, and of credibility within its own constituency, prompted one of the most terrible outrages of the troubles. In November of that year the IRA detonated a bomb at a commemorative service in Enniskillen, killing eleven and injuring sixty-three people in an atrocity that shocked the world.

'This Is Going to Hurt Me . . . ', Heath, *Spectator*, London, 14 November 1987

'*I thought their soccer hooligans were bad enough.*'

'Café Gibraltar', Heath, *Spectator*, London, 14 May 1988

The Enniskillen bomb damaged republican credibility at home and abroad, and reinforced government determination to make the Hillsborough Agreement work. In March 1988, the shooting of three unarmed IRA members in Gibraltar put a great strain on the unity of the Irish and British governments. The deaths also brought fresh allegations from republicans of a shoot-to-kill policy operating in Northern Ireland. The Anglo-Irish Agreement had never been under greater strain.

The Agreement was, however, working after a fashion. Cooperation between governments produced more meaningful cooperation between their police forces, and IRA suspects were more readily and easily extradited from the South to stand trial in the North. To counteract this trend, however, the IRA mounted even bigger and more daring attacks on the security forces and on economic and strategic targets. Over time, a stalemate was reached in the implementation of the Agreement, and stagnation set in. No political initiative was forthcoming from the signatories to keep up a momentum towards a lasting solution. In this political limbo, John Hume, leader of the SDLP, held exploratory talks with the president of Sinn Féin, Gerry Adams. These talks took place in Hume's home city, Derry, early in 1988, and were roundly condemned by unionist politicians and the British government.

'Totality of Relationships', Blotski, *Fortnight*, Belfast, May 1988

Re-arranging the deckchairs

'Re-arranging the deckchairs', Heath, *Spectator*, London, 29 July 1989

In a cabinet reshuffle in July 1989 Thatcher selected a new secretary of state for Northern Ireland, Peter Brooke. Local politicians, most of whom had settled down for the long haul, greeted his arrival with no great enthusiasm. Nothing new was expected by a weary and increasingly cynical population.

'IRA', Heath, *Spectator*, London, 4 August 1990

Brooke attempted to restart the stalled talks towards devolution, as envisaged under the Anglo-Irish Agreement, but was snubbed by unionists. By November 1990 when John Major replaced Margaret Thatcher as leader of the Conservative Party and prime minister, no political progress had been made, and the IRA continued its campaign against leading members of government. In August 1990 Ian Gow, Conservative MP for Eastbourne and close friend of Margaret Thatcher, was killed by a bomb attached to his car.

Early the following year, the IRA continued its campaign against the government by firing mortars at 10 Downing Street when a cabinet meeting was taking place. Not surprisingly, security measures were stepped up to prevent a repeat of such an outrage.

'I'm Sorry Sir . . .', Heath, *Spectator*, London, 9 February 1991

Talks between constitutional parties in Northern Ireland continued throughout 1991, but achieved nothing. In December, Brooke announced that local public spending would be frozen to help defray the increased cost of security. And, as the people of faced into a bleak new year, the IRA blew up a works van at Teebane crossroads near Cookstown, killing seven Protestant workers (an eighth died four days later). That evening, Brooke was a guest on the popular southern Irish talk show, *The Late Late Show*. Unaware of the atrocity, he was cajoled into singing 'My Darling Clementine' to a stunned audience. Unionist opinion was outraged and Brooke offered to resign. His resignation was rejected, but in an April reshuffle he was replaced as secretary of state by Patrick Mayhew.

'Do I know I'm a bloody fool? No! But if you hum it I'll sing it!'

'The Late Late Show', JAK, *Evening Standard*, London, 20 January 1992

Mayhew continued the painstaking search for political accommodation between constitutional parties in Northern Ireland. Concessions were made to the nationalist community when the Ulster Defence Regiment was replaced with the Royal Irish Rifles and the UDA was banned. Talks, however, made little progress and republican terrorist violence continued.

'Advent Calendar', Singleton, *Spectator*, London, 19–26 December 1992

The year 1993 was a depressing one with bombs in Warrington, London, Portadown and Armagh, culminating in the dreadful loss of life on the Shankill Road in Belfast. Ten people were killed and fifty-seven injured when a bomb was detonated in a busy shop on a Saturday morning. Sinn Féin's refusal to condemn the atrocity increased community tension.

Controlled Explosion

'Controlled Explosion', Thompson, *Spectator*, London, 30 October 1993

'The Miracle Worker', Heath, *Spectator*, London, 18–25 December 1993

But developments had been taking place behind the scenes. John Hume and Gerry Adams had continued to meet and to discuss a strategy for a way forward. In September 1993 they issued a joint document to both governments, outlining proposals that would allow Sinn Féin to enter all-party talks on the future of Northern Ireland. An IRA ceasefire was the immediate prerequisite for such an initiative. Initially, Major was dismissive of the proposals, but Hume carried his argument to London and Dublin, and, in December 1993, the Downing Street Declaration was presented to the public by both Major and Taoiseach Albert Reynolds.

'And you can't come to the table . . .', Turner, *Irish Times*, Dublin, 6 January 1994

Unionist response to the joint declaration was hostile. They did not believe that Sinn Féin would adhere to strictly constitutional methods of persuasion. John Hume, too, had to calm fears within his own party, a substantial number of whom feared that he was being used by Sinn Féin for its own ends. Hume insisted on an end to violence before Sinn Féin could be included in talks.

'About Bloody Time', Turner, *Irish Times*, Dublin, 1 September 1994

In August 1994, the IRA declared a complete cessation of military operations, which was swiftly followed by a loyalist ceasefire. Conditions for a political settlement seemed to be in place.

In February 1995 the Framework Documents were issued by the London and Dublin governments. They made clear that Northern Ireland would remain part of the United Kingdom as long as it was the will of the people of Northern Ireland. But they also paved the way for power sharing with nationalists, and provided for the involvement of the Irish Republic in the affairs of Northern Ireland.

'As responsible members . . .', Knox, *Irish News*, Belfast, 23 February 1995

Throughout 1995 implementation of the Framework Documents was put on hold as unionists and republicans wrangled over the issue of the decommissioning of terrorist weapons. Community tension was heightened during the summer as traditional marches were rerouted, and the RUC tried vainly to keep order. As Sinn Féin frustration grew, the IRA rejected the idea of decommissioning.

'Bill Clinton's message . . .', Turner, *Irish Times*, Dublin, 1 December 1995

Untitled, Turner, *Irish Times*, Dublin, 21 February 1996

Constitutional politics was once again the casualty when the IRA dramatically ended its ceasefire and bombed the prestigious Canary Wharf development in London's docklands. Sinn Féin was immediately excluded from talks on the future governance of Northern Ireland.

'Solution No. 3792A', Turner, *Irish Times*, Dublin, 10 June 1996

Government activity in the wake of Canary Wharf led to a new intergovernmental initiative on talks held at Stormont in March 1996. Initially boycotted by the main unionist parties and excluding Sinn Féin, who would not be allowed to join until there was a new IRA ceasefire, the talks made little headway. In May Sinn Féin surprised the political world by agreeing to the Mitchell Principles of non-violent, consensus politics, and were invited to attend the on-going talks. Unionist refusal to sit in the same room as Gerry Adams or Martin McGuinness, the leading Sinn Féin negotiators, produced the farcical situation of separate and simultaneous talks, with a go-between keeping the different factions informed of the thoughts of their adversaries.

'Phew! For a while . . .', Bell, *Guardian*, London, 12 July 1996

Inter-party relations were further damaged during the traditional marching season in Northern Ireland. An Orange Order march, initially blocked from parading down the nationalist Garvaghy Road in Portadown, was subsequently allowed to proceed, a decision that weighed up the potential political fallout, and accepted the theory of proceeding on the basis of the lesser of two evils. Nationalist outrage was total, and long-lasting.

In protest, the SDLP delegation withdrew from the talks process and an uneasy stalemate ensued. The Conservative government in Westminster, led by John Major, was beset with problems of its own. A weak administration, relying on the votes of Ulster Unionists to keep it in power, turned its face against pursuing any immediate solution in Northern Ireland, timidly accepting the status quo. Despite repeated efforts by John Hume, the ailing government refused to act.

'Not just now – I'm busy!', Knox, *Irish News*, Belfast, 30 November 1996

'Frankly, my dear, I do give a damn!', Knox, *Irish News*, Belfast, 22 February 1997

By February 1997, Hume was determined to push for movement on the political front. It was quite clear that the Conservatives could not last much longer, and a Labour administration would be in a stronger position to pursue a meaningful political initiative. In that month, Hume made it clear to the Sinn Féin leadership that if it could not deliver a second and lasting ceasefire, he would look elsewhere for political accommodation.

In May 1997 Labour decisively won the general election called by John Major. Tony Blair became prime minister, and he appointed the charismatic but unpredictable Mo Mowlam as secretary of state for Northern Ireland. A new impetus was given to the search for a solution to the vexed question of how Northern Ireland should be governed. In one of her first speeches, Mowlam indicated that the decommissioning of terrorist weapons would not be allowed to become a stumbling block on the road to all-party talks. Amid on-going community tension over the issue of parades and weapons, the IRA declared a second ceasefire in July 1997, thus allowing Sinn Féin to enter talks.

'Closing Down Sale', Turner, *Irish Times*, Dublin, 19 July 1997

'It's make your mind up time David!', Knox, *Irish News*, Belfast, 31 December 1997

Unionist unease was heightened by Mowlam's unapologetic drive toward an agreed power-sharing solution. Her style of negotiation and her lack of deference caused an on-going deterioration in her relationship with unionist politicians. By the end of the year, David Trimble, recently elected leader of the Ulster Unionist Party and future first minister of Northern Ireland, was presented with a stark choice: either he accept power sharing with nationalists, including Sinn Féin, or he retreat into the age-old strategy of seeking unionist domination of a divided society.

By May 1998, despite continuing sectarian violence and terrorist atrocities, major progress had been made towards a political settlement in Northern Ireland. In April all parties involved in talks signed the Good Friday Agreement, a major breakthrough which would introduce a power-sharing executive. Concessions made to Sinn Féin, including a review of policing, enabled it to change its constitution to allow its members to sit in a Northern Ireland assembly. A referendum on the Good Friday Agreement produced a yes vote of 71.1 per cent in the North and of 94.4 per cent in the South. The Agreement was to produce as many challenges as answers for its signatories.

'The Hand of History', Turner, *Irish Times*, Dublin, 11 April 1998

The distrust which continued to exist between and within communities in Northern Ireland was heightened as the traditional Twelfth of July marches approached. Parades in various parts of Northern Ireland were now being vetted by a Parades Commission, whose every decision was scrutinised by both communities for signs of bias and discrimination. The contentious march to Drumcree parish church, along the nationalist Garvaghy Road in Portadown, was a litmus test for the Commission. When the parade was re-routed in the interests of public safety, the decision was greeted by widespread loyalist violence. This violence culminated in the burning to death of three young brothers – Richard, Mark and Jason Quinn – in a loyalist arson attack on their home in Ballymoney, County Antrim, an action from which the Orange Order was at pains to dissociate itself, but to little avail.

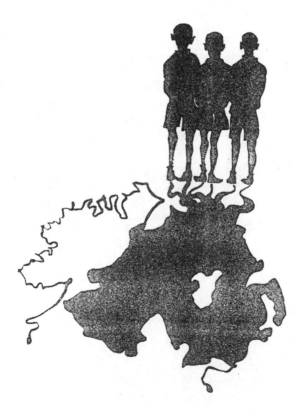

Untitled, McGuiness, *New Statesman*, London, 17 July 1998

One month later a dissident republican terrorist group calling itself the Real IRA detonated a bomb in the centre of Omagh, County Tyrone, on a busy Saturday. The resulting carnage and loss of life – twenty-nine people were killed and over two hundred injured – galvanised politicians into determining that the difficult implementation of the different strands of the Agreement should continue. Public horror and condemnation of the atrocity forced the organisation that had perpetrated the act to cease its operations but, significantly, it did not disband.

'Violent Republicanism', Knox, *Irish News*, Belfast, 22 August 1998

On 14 September 1998 the first meeting of the Northern Ireland Assembly took place at Stormont. Serious questions had still to be answered, most notably the vexed question of decommissioning. Despite this worrying anti-climax, John Hume and David Trimble were awarded the Nobel Peace Prize in October 1998. Debate as to who really deserved such recognition raged throughout the different political constituencies in Northern Ireland.

'Nobel Arms', Knox, *Irish News*, Belfast, 17 October 1998

Unionist insistence on the decommissioning of terrorist weapons, and the IRA's refusal to decommission, dogged political progress. A significant number of the people in Northern Ireland believed that IRA decommissioning was inevitable, and that Sinn Féin must deliver it to ensure its involvement in constitutional politics. But both wings of republicanism steadfastly rejected this call.

'Good Friday Agreement', Simonds, *New Statesman*, London, 9 April 1999

Violent incidents throughout 1999 continued to threaten the fledgling peace process. Mo Mowlam was forced to make a pronouncement on whether punishment beatings and expulsions constituted a breach of the Agreement. Her answer, that they did not, damaged her credibility even further with unionists.

'Last Minute Perrier Entrant . . .', Turner, *Irish Times*, Dublin, 30 August 1999

By the time Tony Blair returned from an ill-fated summer holiday in Tuscany, paid for by Italian taxpayers, the political situation in Northern Ireland was as tense as it had ever been over the past year.

'The Homecoming', Scarfe, *Sunday Times*, London, 5 September 1999

Within a month of his return, Blair replaced Mowlam as secretary of state with Peter Mandelson. Mowlam's credibility with unionists had been further damaged by her welcoming of the Patten Report on the reform of the RUC. Mandelson was seen as an intelligent, effective political mover, close to the prime minister, and someone who would treat sympathetically the susceptibilities of the Ulster unionists. The complexities of politics in Northern Ireland, however, had not eased or diminished because of the selection of a new secretary of state. The continuing debate over the decommissioning of terrorist weapons (especially IRA) turned into a debacle, and Mandelson was forced to suspend the assembly on Friday, 11 February 2000. The suspension was designed to prevent the resignation of its first minister, David Trimble, and to safeguard his increasingly precarious position as Ulster Unionist Party leader.

'Hold It!', Knox, *Irish News*, Belfast, 12 February 2000

In the immediate aftermath of the suspension of the assembly, the IRA withdrew contact with the commission, led by General John de Chastelain, who was charged with overseeing the decommissioning of terrorist weapons. Community tensions grew as the political impasse hardened. Accusation and counter accusation, slur and counter slur were the order of the day: but behind the scenes negotiations were beginning to happen. These were made more difficult by the recommendations of the Independent Commission on Policing, specifically the proposed change to the name of the RUC. On his return from Washington, after attending the St Patrick's Day celebrations, David Trimble was met with a leadership challenge. At the annual meeting of the UUP, the Reverend Martin Smyth, MP for South Belfast and former grand master of the Orange Order in Ireland, gained 43 per cent of the vote against David Trimble, an inadequate but effective challenge by anti-Agreement unionists.

'Funny New World', Turner, *Irish Times*, Dublin, 28 March 2000

Pressure now mounted to have the assembly put back in place. Meetings in Belfast, London, Dublin and Hillsborough took place between politicians, civil servants, political advisers, spin doctors and anyone who could help in moving the process forward. By early May 2000, Peter Mandelson was able to report substantial progress. Renewed promises of movement on IRA decommissioning led him to propose a reinstatement of the assembly on 22 May. This placed David Trimble in a difficult position: not only did he have to agree to reinstatement without actual IRA decommissioning, he also had to sell this to his party.

'Coming Soon', Turner, *Irish Times*, Dublin, 23 May 2000

Despite real misgivings and a very narrow majority – 47 per cent of the Ulster Unionist Council rejected a proposed return – David Trimble succeeded in persuading his party to rejoin the assembly. In doing so, and in what some believed was a thowaway line to appease unionist hardliners, he attacked Sinn Féin saying they needed to be 'house trained' before they could become bona fide democrats. This school yard rhetoric incensed Sinn Féin. It also highlighted the real political and psychological gap that exists between unionism and nationalism in Northern Ireland.

'It was the dogs in the street . . .', Knox, *Irish News*, Belfast, 29 May 2000

That gap received full media scrutiny during the Orange celebrations in July 2000. Still angry at being prevented from marching down the predominantly nationalist Garvaghy Road, the protest by orangemen at Drumcree church in Portadown, County Armagh, was now in its fourth year. Community tension throughout Northern Ireland was heightened by calls from Portadown Orange Lodge for supporters to organise street demonstrations in an attempt to reverse the Parades Commission decision. The inevitable violence that ensued, directed against the army and the RUC, was less than in previous years, but the refusal of the Portadown Orange Lodge leader, Harold Gracey, to condemn the violence brought home to a world audience the continuing and unresolved divisions in Northern Ireland. It also highlighted the challenge faced by politicians of every hue in their search for a workable future for Northern Ireland.

'Orange Traditions No. 35', Turner, *Irish Times*, Dublin, 15 July 2000